ST. BRIDES MAJOR, SOUTHERNDOWN AND OGMORE-BY-SEA

ST. BRIDES MAJOR, SOUTHERNDOWN AND OGMORE-BY-SEA

A CHRONICLE OF A PARISH
IN THE VALE OF GLAMORGAN

BY
STANLEY W. BEVAN

Best Wishes

Stanley. W. Bevan

1980
D. BROWN & SONS LTD.,
COWBRIDGE & BRIDGEND

© S. BEVAN

ISBN 0 905928 11 3

This book is dedicated to my wife Mary and to my daughter Patricia, in appreciation of the help and inspiration they have given me in writing it.

The author acknowledges the help of Dr. John Howden of the Glamorgan Heritage Coast Project and Mr Mark Coleman in the preparation of the cover design.

Printed and designed by D. Brown & Sons Ltd., Cowbridge & Bridgend

Contents

List of Illustrations

Autobiography

I was born at Pool Cottage, St. Brides Major, on the 26th of September 1900, the same cottage where my father was born, and died. I was the youngest of the family of four girls. My mother was born in Arbroath, County Angus, Scotland and came to London by sea, sailing from Dundee, to become a housemaid to the Dunraven family in their London home and later transferred to Dunraven Castle.

We were a very happy family, poor from a money point of view, but rich in affection for our parents. When we were growing up I remember my mother telling us 'times were hard when you children were little, your father's money was only seven and twenty (shillings) and only enough for bread and leather.'

My father, a stone mason, started work when he was ten years old. He told me that, when he went to work with his father at Plas Llanfihangel, near Cowbridge, owned by the Dunraven Estate, they would take food to last them the week. He would run alongside the donkey, holding on to the harness while his father rode with the week's supply of food. He never forgot having to sleep in a part of the house which had at one time been used to imprison wrongdoers and being homesick often cried himself to sleep. Having to work at such an early age my father had very little schooling and therefore was not a good scholar, but was a first-class stone mason and much of his work is still to be seen in the area. He was a fluent Welshman, but my mother being Scottish, there was very little Welsh spoken in the home.

My father and mother were staunch Church people and my sisters and myself were brought up to follow their example. In those days the Sabbath day in the parish was truly a Holy Day; Church service in the morning, Sunday school in the afternoon, and service in the evening and it was looked upon as wicked even to whistle on Sunday. Our shoes had to be cleaned ready for Church on Saturday night, my father would cut the cabbage and bring in the potatoes and sticks and coal for the morning.

All through my boyhood days I always had the desire to go to sea, this may have been in my blood, as all the male side of my mother's family were connected with the sea; so at the age of thirteen I made up my mind to try my luck. By selling rabbits which were poached, and doing any odd

7

Pool Cottage, home of the Bevan family for over 200 years.

THE BEVAN FAMILY GROUP, 1908.
Isabella, Mother, Florence, Father, Emily.
Seated: Stanley, Dorothy.

jobs which came my way, I saved enough money for my train fare to Barry. There, at the docks I tried several ships for a job without success. On one I was told 'go home to your mother', this brought me down to earth and I returned home a saddened but a much wiser boy.

I now realised I had to face my mother and admit that she had been right. When I told her that I was running away she had said 'Go you my boy, I don't think you will find a better place than this.' Many years afterwards I had cause to remember her wise words on many occasions.

Arriving back in Bridgend I started to walk home to St. Brides and, in a secondhand shop in Nolton Street, I saw in the window a pile of gramophone records, priced sixpence each. Now, we had a gramophone at home and I had exactly sixpence left in my pocket, so I had the brilliant idea of taking a peace offering home to my mother. I went into the shop and was told that you could not choose a record from the pile, but had to take them as they came off the top, so I took one and continued my walk home.

I well remember my mother's face as I entered the house, there was no 'I told you so', but a cooked dinner was put on the table in my usual place. I then shamefacedly presented her with my peace offering. With tongue in cheek she thanked me and said we would all hear it after we had eaten. My father had finished his dinner, sat back and lit his pipe, and we all settled down to hear the new record. It was half way through when I realised the significance of its title; it was 'I'll be with you when the roses bloom again', and after this every time the record was played it raised a laugh. It was often played for many years, because it was a lovely song, but my sisters never let me live it down.

The next time I left home was during the first World War, for military service, I was seventeen years of age, and I will never forget the time when I was saying goodbye to my mother at the front gate, with tears on her cheeks she kissed me and said, 'I am proud of you, Stan.'

Shortly after leaving school I was apprenticed to the plumbing trade in the leading ironmonger's workshop of D. E. Evans, Dunraven Place, Bridgend. The conditions on the form my parents' signed, were that I would not be allowed to marry, not to enter a public house, and the hours of work would be from 8 a.m. to 7 p.m. (with one hour for dinner) 8 a.m. to 1 p.m. on Saturday. Wages were two shillings and sixpence for the first year, five shillings per week for the second year, seven shillings and sixpence for the third year and ten shillings for the fourth year. There were two unpaid holidays each year, Good Friday and Christmas Day.

Looking back over the years, these conditions were hard on a young-ster like myself—having to cycle home to St. Brides in all kinds of weather—and it also meant that I was always too late to take part in any of the village activities, concerts etc. Nevertheless I am grateful to this day for the training I received with this firm, which included plumbing, gasfitting, tinsmith, locksmith, domestic heating and house drainage. This firm also undertook the work of retinning copper cooking utensils and would collect these articles from all the large houses in the area. As a boy the preparation work fell upon me, and, using spirits of salts, great care had to be taken to avoid breathing in the fumes. It was also my job to wrap them in tissue to avoid marking the highly polished inside. No one was allowed into the workshop when this work was carried out and great secrecy was maintained, as this process was known to very few at that time, I can safely say that I am the only one in South Wales who knows the coveted ancient process.

My first year of apprenticeship passed and I went into the office to receive my first rise in wages and was paid with a five-shilling piece, which was usual in those days. On my arrival home that evening I proudly presented to my mother the five-shilling piece, feeling proud of my advancement. She was delighted with my progress into the industrial world, as she put it, and upon examining the coin, said 'What a coinci-dence, it is dated 1900, the year of your birth, take it and keep it yourself and treasure it.' This I have done and it is a beautiful memory among my souvenirs.

Little did I know then that I would realise my life's ambition to own my own house. In March 1936, I took the plunge and bought a plot of a quarter of an acre of land in the centre of the village from Mr R. W. Hopkins of Tynyporth Farm and made up my mind to do all the work in-volved myself. With difficulty I surveyed the plot, drew plans which were acceptable to my wife and I, and submitted them to the Glamorgan County Council and to the District Council for acceptance. Permission was granted, the plans were passed, and I commenced the work by cut-ting the first turf. I then did the labouring, excavating and concreting the foundations. Then came the bricking which was done with Bryncethin bricks throughout, up to the roof level. I cut the roof timbers by measurement on the ground with the exception of the hip blades. I could not afford to make a mistake with these as they measured 25 feet of 9″ by 3″ so by using a template this was overcome. Slating and lead flashing came next, this finished, it enabled me to work independent of the weather to lay the floors in T & G floorboards. Now came the interior work of first fixing carpentry and the rendering of plaster, followed by the second carpentry work of fixing skirting, picture rail, plate rail and architrave on windows and doors. The plumbing and electrical work being completed, I then commenced the interior decorating and outdoor painting. I now had the satisfaction of being able to say I built the house myself singlehanded.

A Horse called Picton

At the entrance to Blackhall Road and at the rear of the Farmers' Arms, was Shop Farm, a two-storey thatched cottage with farm yard and buildings attached. This farm had been in the occupation of the Hopkin family for generations, the last of the line was Miss Tabitha Hopkin, who was the great aunt of Lord Ogmore.

Miss Hopkin kept a herd of cows and sold milk and cheese to her village customers, I well remember as a boy, going into her dairy and seeing the cheese in the press and the fresh milk in earthenware pans standing on the cold slate benches and watching her skimming off the cream with her round dished skimmer.

Living with my parents next door in Pool Cottage, I used to spend a lot of time helping Miss Hopkin, turning the churn until the butter was made and watch her patting it into shape with the white wood hand patters leaving the final imprint of a cow or a sheaf of corn. For my assistance I would be rewarded with a bakestone cake and a small can of milk to take home. The butter milk left in the churn after the butter had been removed, was in great demand for making 'Teisen Lap' a prince amongst Welsh cakes, it was also given to her customers for feeding calves and pigs.

In the evening Miss Hopkin would come into our house for a chat with my mother and father and would sit on the little settle near the fire. Although Miss Hopkin was Welsh speaking, she never spoke in Welsh to my father, respecting my mother's Scottish birth.

Miss Hopkin owned only one horse called Picton and everyone knew and loved old Picton. He could be hired for a modest fee and was in great demand throughout the village for ploughing the large gardens and hauling the harvested fern from the common. The fern was used for bedding in the pigsty, found in practically every house garden in the village. It was a common sight to see a mow of fern, thatched with reeds from the river, standing in a corner of the garden near the pigsty; it also provided a useful supply of garden manure.

Every Saturday morning Miss Hopkin would journey to Bridgend to do her weekly shopping and it was my job to bring Picton from the field, groom him, oil his hooves, polish the harness brasses, put him in the trap and bring the outfit around to the front door of the cottage. Miss Hopkin would come out with her baskets and rug, and climb up into the trap. I would wrap the rug around her legs, lift my cap and off would trot Picton.

About four o'clock in the afternoon I would be on the lookout for the return of Miss Hopkin. I would carry her baskets and rug into the house, take the trap around into the yard, feed and water Picton and return him to the field with a bundle of hay. I would then return to the house to collect my pay, which was sixpence, a plate of Welsh cakes, and a can of milk. At the age of ten, this was considered a fair return for my labour.

With reference to the paragraph above, relating to Picton the horse, I wrote to Lord Ogmore, telling him of the story of his Great Aunt and Picton. He replied expressing his thanks and stated that he contributed some of his writings to the *London Welshman*. He sent me a copy, which stated that his forebears who farmed at Coity, moved the entire household and stock. Lord Ogmore had a great affection for the parish and the surrounding district, having lived in Bridgend with his parents and remembered his Great Aunt and Picton.

The following is the reply I received from Lord Ogmore:

HOUSE OF LORDS

27th November 1968.

Dear Mr Bevan,

Thank you for your letter and for letting me read your note regarding Miss Tabitha Hopkin and Picton. I read this with great interest.

I was also interested to hear that you are writing a book about the Parish of St Brides Major.

In addition to the article you mention in your letter, I also wrote two articles for the *London Welshman* in January and February 1967, the former contains some stories of St Brides and if it would interest you, I would be pleased to send you a copy.

With best wishes for 1969.

Yours sincerely,

OGMORE

Dad's Army

In the early part of the 1914-18 war, a Home Defence Corps was formed in the parish, called the V.T.C. (Voluntary Training Corps) of which my father was a member. It was made of old men who were too old for the regular forces, and did duty guarding various places, such as the docks, gasworks, power stations etc., and thereby relieving regular soldiers who were badly needed for service overseas.

Looking back over the years, one cannot help admiring these grand old men, whilst seeing the humorous side, and I can only liken them to Dad's Army as seen on television today.

The St. Brides Major Section consisted of approximately forty men, under the command of Mr H. O. Irvine, agent for the Dunraven Estate, holding the rank of Captain. He was supported by one Sergeant, Mr Hopkin Jones, of the Merthyrmawr Estate, and four Corporals—The Rev. Thomas Watkins, Mr Thomas Hadden, Mr Walter Symes and Mr Thomas Hopkin, the well known Bisley marksman.

The Headquarters was the long room of the Farmers' Arms and the parade ground was the village green opposite.

They were equipped with an arm band and a wooden rifle with which they did their preliminary training.

I was nearly seventeen at the time and having failed to enter the army, owing to my age, I followed the V.T.C. and watched with envy hoping that one day I would be able to join the 'Old Crocks', as they were affectionately called. Eventually, after quite an amount of pleading, I was enrolled as a member on the understanding that my term of service would end on my attaining the age of eighteen, when I would be eligible for the regular army. On the next weekly parade I was issued with an arm band and a wooden rifle and fell in alongside my father. At last I had achieved my ambition to become a soldier, I was in 'Dad's Army'.

The great day arrived when we were told that we were to be given uniforms and members were instructed to produce their measurements at the next parade and I am sure that some of the measuring was done with a school ruler or an elastic tape measure, because when the bundles of clothing were delivered a great deal of exchanging had to be done to obtain a fairly good fit.

As the last recruit to join I had to have what was left, which would have fitted a superman, but thanks to my mother's skill, she being an

13

Private William Bevan, father of the writer in the uniform of 'Dad's Army', 2nd Battalion, V.B. the Welch Regiment.

MEMBERS OF 'DAD'S ARMY', 1917.
Back Row: Privates—T. Williams, C. Parkin, S. W. Bevan, Cpl. T. Hadden.
Seated: Q.M.Sgt. Davies, Lt. H. O. Irvine, Sgt. P. Crowden.

ST. BRIDES MAJOR,
MEMBERS OF THE 2nd LINE GLAMORGANSHIRE YEOMANRY, 1914
Back Row: R. Harry, W. J. Bevan, J. Rees, B. David, H. David, E. Wheeler, E. Hopkin. *Middle Row:* I.
Hopkin, J. Sharrat, S. Richards, F. Hayden, A. Bevan, T. Williams, W. Williams. *Front Row:* T.
Bevan, F. Davies, R. Smith, E. Williams, T. Hardee, A. Bowen.

expert with the needle, a reasonable fit was obtained. It took a long time for some of the men to master the art of rolling on their putties securely and it was a common sight to see a man when marching, come to a sudden stop because his putties had become undone and had been stepped on by the man following behind and throwing the whole column into disorder.

Guard duties were shared by various detachments throughout Glamorgan and in due course our turn came. With five old men and myself we reported to Dumfries Drill Hall, Cardiff, where we were issued leather equipment, an Enfield rifle and a clip of 303 ammunition. Under the command of corporal Rev. Thomas Watkins, we journeyed to Cardiff and down to the docks by tram and reported to the guardroom which was an old railway carriage. This was the real thing, and we did sentry duty alongside the dark open quay. At 2 a.m. my turn came and with fear and trembling I marched along my beat on the quay, deriving comfort from my loaded rifle and feeling a real soldier at last. Dawn came and including my two hours on duty I have not closed my eyes all night, but I slept in the tram to the station and in the train to Bridgend, then walked the four miles home.

At a later date all detachments were ordered to attend a parade at the Dumfries Drill Hall, Cardiff, where we were inspected by a 'Brass Hat' of the regular army, who told us what wonderful work we were doing and called for volunteers for guard duty on the East Coast.

This was a chance to further my ambition, I took one pace forward and stood smartly to attention, and how I prayed that I would be accepted! My prayer was answered and I was told to report back in a week's time, for new uniform and full kit. This I did and with several others of which I was by far the youngest, we were sent as a detachment to the Glamorgan Yeomanry, 2/1 line stationed at Worlingham Camp, Beccles, Suffolk. Although the Yeomanry were horse mounted we were given bicycles. Many of our men had never ridden a bicycle, but the numerous spills and pile-ups were eventually overcome.

We did duty on the coast at Benacre Beach, in trenches and dugouts, but unfortunately the dugouts were the headquarters for swarms of mosquitoes which played havoc if you slept with your face or hands uncovered. I was learning fast! I remember one morning seeing a man emerge from a dugout with both his eyes completely closed, a mosquito victim.

During our training we were sent to a town called Witham, North London, to fire our musketry course. I had been rifle shooting—air rifle, .22, and service rifle—since I was ten years old, taught by Mr T. Hopkin, now Corporal Hopkin. This paid off as I came through the course with the highest score and I felt very proud when the Colonel read out the result on the parade ground; I was now a marksman and entitled to wear on my left sleeve crossed guns and a star. No Brigadier was more proud of his baton than I was of my crossed guns and star.

I had reason to thank 'Dad's Army' for quite a lot, especially later on in my real army life. I was now nearly eighteen years old and I was given my discharge to await my calling-up papers for the armed forces. I treasure today the discharge paper, together with my father's which is in the form of a letter of thanks, and signed by Sir Winston Churchill. I later served with the Welch Regiment in France, Belgium, Germany and Ireland and was discharged on the Curragh in Ireland in 1919 with the rank of Acting Company Sergeant Major.

I credit my rapid promotion to the all round training I received in 'Dad's Army'. There is a sequel to this story. In 1974, I received a telephone call from a Mrs Marley of Cheltenham stating that she was the daughter of the late Mr H. O. Irvine of Southerndown and would like to meet me. This was arranged and while staying at Little West, Southerndown, she called at my home. She explained that her sister who had lived at Weston-Super-Mare, had died and among her effects was a silver bowl and also a post card photograph of the men who had won it, including her father, whilst serving in the 2nd Battalion V.T.C. the Welch Regiment. From the names on the back of the photograph she had traced me

Silver Bowl won by the above group of 'Dad's Army'.

and being the only living member of the team, she thought it fitting that the bowl should be returned to its original home, 55 years after the platoon had won it. It now occupies a place among my souvenirs.

The Parish

St. Brides Major appears to have been the forgotten or cinderella corner of Glamorgan, but I have always looked upon it with pride as the gateway to the Garden of Wales, the beautiful Vale of Glamorgan.

St. Brides Major was named after St. Bridget who was born in Ireland in 453 A.D. and is reported to have stayed in the village.

It must be remembered that prior to 1920 there was no such place as Ogmore-by-Sea as it was then part of Southerndown known as Sutton, taking its name from the celebrated Sutton Stone Quarries.

The Parish Council was represented by seven members of the Community. Permission was granted by the Glamorgan County Council to divide the Parish into three Wards—St. Brides Major, Southerndown and Ogmore-by-Sea.

In the year 1871 the population of	Southerndown was	324
	St. Brides Major	307
	Total	631
In the year 1965 the population of	Southerndown was	250
	St. Brides Major	725
	Ogmore-by-Sea	900
	Total	1875
In the year 1975-76 the Parish Population was		2000
	Electorate	1400
	Councillors	10

At the lower end of the village of St. Brides Major, are three groups of trees, planted on the Common alongside the Bridgend road. The lower group of chestnut trees were planted to commemorate the departure of General Picton to the Battle of Waterloo. General Picton having stayed at Tyn-y-caeau Farm nearby prior to his departure into battle.

In December 1937 a group of trees were planted to commemorate the Coronation of King George VI. This is recorded in the Royal Book of Commemorative Tree Planting throughout the British Empire and part of the United States.

In December 1969, twenty one trees were planted by dignataries and young people of the Parish to mark the 21st birthday of Prince Charles and his Investiture as The Prince of Wales. Three of the trees (Silver Birch) represent the three Wards of the Parish, and is another chapter in the parochial history of the village.

Parish Council Chain of Office

Each year the members of the St. Brides Major Parish Council (now the Community Council) together with their wives and husbands meet for dinner. The year 1965 was a special one, in that the Parish Council was a special one, the Parish Council was presented on behalf of Lady Burbridge with a Chairman's Badge of Office, the design of which represents local interests.

Lady Burbridge gave the Badge of Office to the Parish in memory of her mother Mrs. Alice Moxey who had lived and spent many happy days in the Parish.

Lady Burbridge was unable to be present to make the presentation and Mr Wilfred Powell, (Clerk to the Parish Council) acted on her behalf.

After the presentation District Councillor Harry Price J.P., Chairman of Penybont Rural District Council, invested Councillor R. E. Pearce, Chairman of the St. Brides Major Parish Council, with the Badge of Office.

ST. BRIDES MAJOR PARISH COUNCIL, 1964-1965
Standing: G. Garrett, A. Stone, M. Jenkins, A. Davies, S. W. Bevan, D. Battrick, W. Powell. *Seated:* E. Loveluck, D. Hopkin, R. Pearce, D. C. H. Price (Chairman District Council), D. L. Heard.

Parish Boundary

Commencing where the Alun River enters the Ewenny River near Ty Maen Farm, it follows the River Alun through Park Wood to the Ford and Stepsau Ddion. On to the old stone slab bridge at Pont-y-Brown past the old Southerndown Road railway station and Croes Cwta Farm to the North Lodge of Cleminstone and continues on to Picket Farm and Church Farm near the boundary of Llandow.

Returning back to the Cleminstone brook it crosses the Wick to Ewenny road, then overland to a point near Cae Caradoc Farm, crosses the Wick to St. Brides road at Cae Caradoc Cross following the Broughton road to a point near Maes Isah Farm then overland in a south westerly direction to the cliff to Dunraven Park and Castle grounds to the foreshore at Dunraven Bay continuing along the Common past Southerndown to Ogmore-by-Sea and river mouth.

General view of the centre of the village.

General view of the lower end of the village, showing Pant.

The Pool and Pitcot, 1910.

Follow the river past Portabello to the stepping stones at Ogmore Castle crossing over the moors to Merthyr Mawr Suspension Bridge. Then across the Moors to the White Bridge and the Watermill and back to Ty Maen Farm.

St. Brides Major Conservation Area

A large expanding village, three miles south of Bridgend. The conservation area lies on either side of the B4265 east of its junction with B4524 road from Southerndown. It extends in linear form, rising gently to the crest of the low wooded ridge to the east of the village. The area is predominantly agricultural in character, with informal groups of cottages and farm buildings scattered along the road, either on the road, either on the roadside or set back behind small informal greens. At its lower point the road skirts a large village pond, before entering a fine grove of trees near the road junction. The pond and its associated green overlooked by an inn (The Farmers' Arms), farm and cottages, forms the focal point of the area.

The buildings are well cared for and are generally of stone with slated roofs. Two groups in particular are good examples of their period and are listed as buildings of architectural and historic interest. The area

21

owes much of its visual quality to the colour and texture of the local stone used in the buildings and also in the lichen covered field and boundary walls along the roadway between the two groups. The area's pleasant special qualities are reflected in its buildings and environment.

Footways—Bridle Ways—Driftways

There are fortytwo right-of-ways within the Parish Boundary, and some of these rank among the finest in the Principality. Come with me along some of these paths so that you may at a future date enjoy what our forefathers have handed down to us.

The mouth of the river Ogmore is the north western point of the boundary. Following the river inland you pass Portabello House, on to where the river Ewenny joins the river Ogmore and on to the steps of St. Teilo (stepping stones) then travel along a track or bridle-way to the ford and suspension bridge (swing bridge) at Merthyr Mawr, returning over a stile across the moors to a concrete bridge joining the main road near the Mid Glamorgan Water Board pumping station. Then along the main road past the Ogmore Water Mill to Ty Maen Farm.

Then entering a miniature valley called the Rhiw you come up to the common near the 14th Green of the Southerndown Golf Club. Here you have before you one of the finest views in Glamorgan. To the west overlooking Porthcawl is the Swansea bay, the Uplands of Swansea, the Mumbles, and fading into the backround the blue outline of the Gower Coast.

Turning to the right inland, you see Margam Mynydd, the Llynfi, Garw and Ogmore valleys. Looking down you can see the thatched roofed cottages of Merthyr Mawr village peering through the trees. Further along you see the wooded area above Pencoed and Brynna, the Garth mountain, Llantrisant, and, in the distance the Caerphilly mountain. Looking toward the sea southwards (visibility permitting) you can see the Somerset coast from Minehead to the Doone Valley, Porlock, Lynmouth, Combe Martin and fading into the distance Ilfracombe and Bull Point. Nearer home you can see the Vale of Glamorgan including Colwinstone, the stacks of the Leys Electricity Power Station, and the clumps of trees on top of Stalling Down, Cowbridge, known as Primrose Hill, where, it is said, the last man in Wales was hung in Public.

Return to St. Brides Major village across Ogmore Down via Heol-y-Millwr then climb Sionis Hill to Blackhall Road where you may take a pathway which will lead you to the lane taking you past the Daffodil Wood (Coed-y-Bwl), which in Spring is carpeted with wild daffodils. Passing this wood you come to the river Alun over which is a lovely old slab footbridge (now classed as an ancient monument). This footpath carries a right-of-way over the railway and into the Ewenny boundary to Wallace Farm.

About fifty yards past the old footbridge is a driftway leading up to the Old Castle Down. This driftway allows sheep to come down from the Common to the river to drink.

Continue alongside the river under the railway bridge you see before you the Alun Valley with the wooded slope of Ewenny Park. On your right are the hazel and oak trees of Ysgubur-y-Warren. On the left hazel nuts abound and the village children enjoy picking these in late August or early September. In this valley may be seen lovely specimens of wild bird life but unfortunately the rock blasting in a nearby quarry has driven much of the wild life further along the valley. But now the quarrying has ceased it is noted that the wild life has returned.

Travelling in a northerly direction along the valley you come to the Ford and Stepping Stones known as Stepsau Ddion. Crossing the river here you enter the Ewenny Parish into a lane leading to County Ewenny-Wick Road, which the old legend describes as the Starving Rascal. This unusual title deserves an explanation.

Apparently an old destitute tramp travelling from Bridgend towards Wick had called at a farm above Ewenny Pottery and asked for a drink and begged for food. This was refused him so he cursed the farmer and called the place Mount Misery. The rascal travelled through Ewenny and along the road mentioned and called at another farm about two miles further on, here again he made his request for food and drink. The farmer or his wife, either from fear or pity, gave him the food and drink asked for. The man now refreshed, blessed the people and the farm and named it Mount Pleasant, and it is still known by this name to the present day.

Leaving the Ford and Stepping Stones you follow the river under the railway arch and here again another part of the valley is revealed. Wood slopes on either side and the river meandering through lush grassland and disappearing into further woodland. Climbing the wooded slope brings you to the highest point of Old Castle Down overlooking the village of St. Brides Major and continues on down to the Blackhall Road near Groes Anthony.

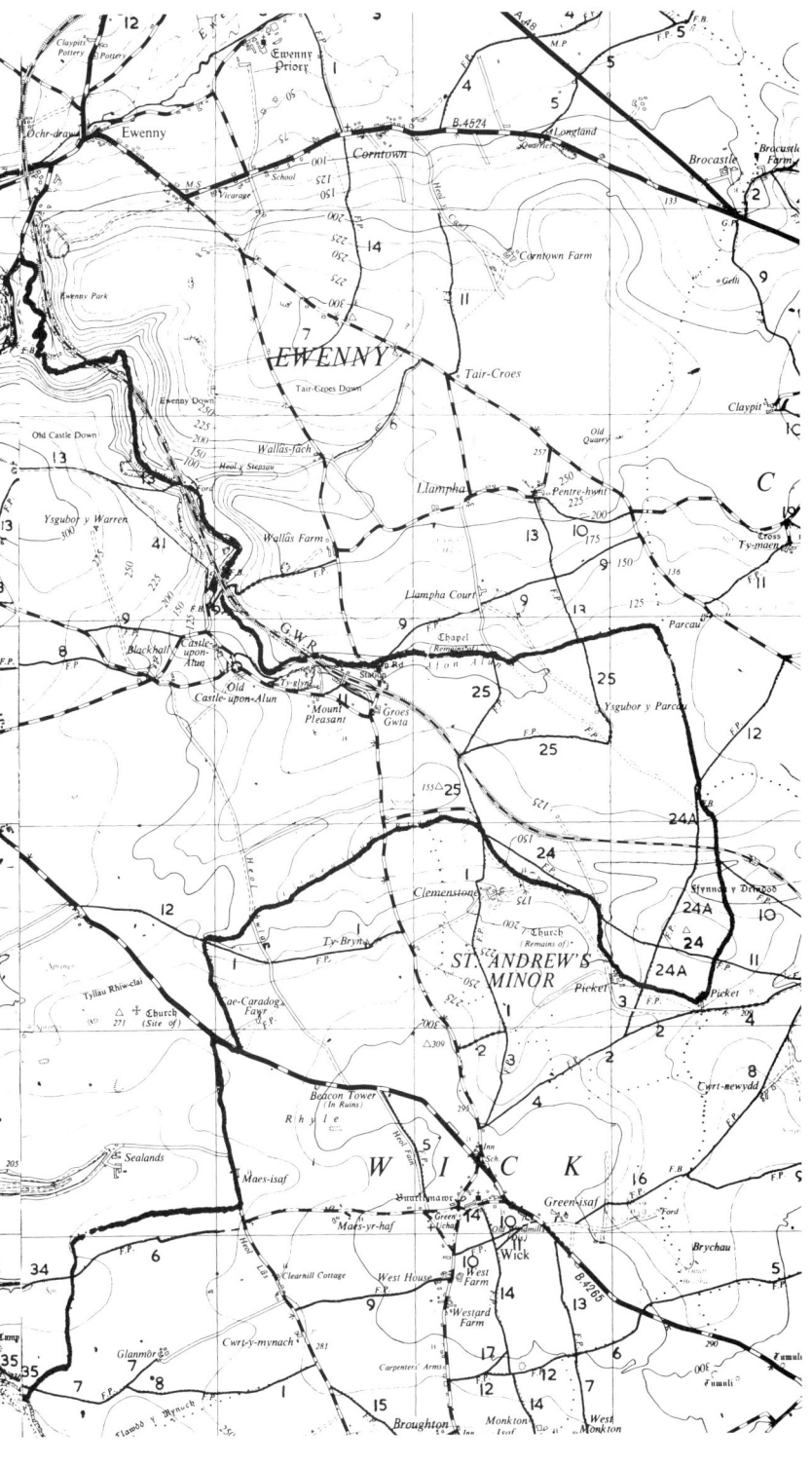

Footpath No. 17 commences at Pitcot Green opposite the Farmers' Arms, over the fields of Pool Farm and ending on the highway near Great House, Southerndown. One of these fields deserves a mention. This is a field where the footpath runs right through the middle from stile to stile, and being arable land is ploughed in the proper season. Living in a cottage in Pitcot was a family by the name of Curtis. George Curtis, the father, worked at Slade Farm, Southerndown and walked to work in all weathers using footpath 17. When the field had been ploughed up by the farmer George would be the one to break the trail for the new path across the freshly ploughed ground. It was always noted by the locals who frequently used this path if George had wandered or had stuck to the straight and narrow because the path as George made it remained until the next ploughing.

Another pathway starting from the same stile as No. 17 travels across several fields to the top of Slade Wood which is entered by a 'kissing gate', then down through the wood along-side Dunraven Park wall and ending near the Seamouth Cafe at Dunraven Bay.

Rights of Way

Definitions

The terms used in these notes are given the following meanings by the National Parks and Access to the Countryside Act, 1949.

Footpath;
> means a highway over which the public have a right of way on foot only, other than such a highway at the side of a public road.

Bridleway;
> means a highway over which the public have a right of way on foot and a right of way on horse-back or leading a horse, with or without a right to drive animals along the highway. In 1968 cycles were permitted to be used on Bridleways giving way to a horse. In 1970 invalid carriages were also allowed.

Public Path;
> means a highway being either a footpath or a bridleway.

Road Used as a Public Path;
means a highway, other than a public path, used by the public mainly for the purposes for which footpaths or bridleways are so used.

Access to the Countryside

1. *Footpath* Commences on the bank of the River Ogmore near the swing bridge, Merthyr Mawr and proceeds southwest across fields to cross the Ewenny River over concrete footbridge to terminate on the County Road west of the Water Works. 450 yards

2. *Bridleway* Commences at the end of the County Road on the Rhiw; proceeds southwards on to the old Heol-y-Milwyr across Ogmore Down, crossing bridleways 36, 21, and 30 to the junction of bridleways 28, 29 and CRF 28 at the southern edge of the Down. 1650 yards.

3. *Bridleway* Commences on a lane to the rear of the Pelican Inn, Ogmore; proceeds southwards across Ogmore Down to cross bridleway 26, and Heol-y-Slough to terminate on the County Road northeast of Heol-y-Mynydd. 1900 yards.

4. *Footpath* Commences on the Norton Hall—Groes Road and proceeds eastwards across a field to a County Road northwest of Heol-y-Mynydd. 250 yards.

5. *Footpath* Commences at the junction bridleway 26 on Heol-y-Slough and proceeds eastwards across fields passing south of Ty'n-y-Caeau Farm to the junction of CRF 28 near the remains of Croes Antoni. 950 yards.

6. *Footpath* Commences on Heol-y-Slough west of Bull Hill road junction and proceeds northwards across fields to the lane leading from the County Road to Ty'n-y-Fynwent. Closed on 5th June, 1965. 520 yards.

7. *Footpath* Commences at the junction of footpath No. 6 on Heol-y-Slough and proceeds northeast across a field to terminate on the County Road opposite old School now diverted around new School. 320 yards.

8. *Footpath* Commences on a County Road opposite rear of old School in lane on Penylan Road; proceeds eastwards along the lane and across fields to terminate on the crossroads at Blackhall. 1200 yards.

27

9. *Footpath* Commences on a County Road northwest of Blackhall and proceeds eastwards across fields to terminate on the County road at the southern end of Coed-y-Bwl. 55 yards.

9a *Footpath* Commences on the County Road crossing Pont-y-Brown and proceeds northeast to the Parish boundary on the Afon Alun, over the stone slab footbridge. 60 yards.

10. *Footpath* Commences on the County Road between Castle-upon-Alun and Old Castle-upon-Alun; proceeds southeast across a field at the rear of the castle site and turns southwest at Pant to terminate on the County Road. 320 yards.

11. *Footpath* Commences on the County Road opposite Mount Pleasant and proceeds northeast to a footbridge over the railway near the goods shed, turning southeast across a field, past a cattle pen to the station approach road. Continues on the opposite side of the approach road and terminates on the County Road north of Groes Gwta Farm. *Closed on 31st May, 1968.* 300 yards.

12. *Footpath* Commences on the County Road near the private road junction of Pant-y-Groes Lodge and proceeds southeast across fields to the Parish boundary west of Ffynnon Shwlac on Heol-Shwlac. 750 yards.

13. *Bridleway* Commences on the County Road at Croes Antoni and proceeds northwards along the eastern edge of the Common past Bryn-awel. Continues eastwards across Graig-Ddu turning north to pass under the railway alongside the river, thence southwards to terminate on the County Road and Parish boundary near Stepsau Dduon. 1700 yards.

14. *Bridleway* Commences at Groes Farm on the Southerndown Road and proceeds west and then due south along a lane to terminate on the County Road east of Little West House, Southerndown. (Green Lane.) 875 yards.

15. *Footpath* Commences on the County Road east of Little West House and proceeds eastwards across fields to terminate on the County Road north of Dunlop Cottage, Southerndown. 480 yards.

16. *Footpath* Commences on the County Road opposite Southern-down Farm proceeds southeast across fields to Slade and continues down into Slade Wood to junction with footpath 18 near Dunraven Laundry. (Seamouth Cafe.) 700 yards.

17. *Footpath* Commences on the County road in Southerndown north of Ty-Mawr (Great House) and proceeds east and northeast across fields to terminate on the County Road in Pitcott opposite the Farmer's Arms Inn. 1650 yards.

18. *Footpath* Commences on footpath 17 behind pitcot Green; and proceeds southwest for a short distance across fields turning into

Slade Wood and along the western edge of Dunraven Park to the County Road and the beach at Dunraven Bay. 1800 yards.

19. *Bridleway* Commences on a lane to the rear of the Pelican Inn; proceeds northeast for a short distance before turning southeast across Ogmore Down to run down the eastern edge of enclosed land (allotments) and then southwest along the boundary of the enclosed land. Continues across bridleway 26 to terminate on Heol-y-Slough opposite the road leading to Heol-y-Mynydd. 2500 yards.

20. *Bridleway* Commences on the County road at the Rhiw and proceeds southwest across Ogmore Down to the junction of Bridleway 19. 600 yards.

21. *Bridleway* Commences at Pant St. Brides; proceeds westwards across Ogmore Down along Rhiw Forgan, then south-west, crossing bridleway 2 (Heol-y-Milwyr) and 30 to the junction of bridleways 19 and 29. 1000 yards.

22. *Bridleway* Commences at the junction of Bridleway 23 at the southern tip of King's Wood and proceeds southwest across Ogmore Down to the junction of Bridleway 21 at the turn of Rhiw Forgan. 750 yards.

22a *Footpath* Commences at Pant St. Brides opposite the wooded part of Ewenny Park, proceeds westwards to the top of Ogmore Down crossing Bridleway 22 and continuing north west to the junction with Bridleway 23. 400 yards.

23. *Bridleway* Commences at the junction of Bridleway 22 at the southern tip of King's Wood and proceeds westward along the northern edge of Ogmore Down passing south of a reservoir to junction with Bridleway 2. 950 yards.

24. *Footpath* Commences on the County road opposite Clementstone North Lodge and proceeds across fields crossing Footpath 24a to the parish boundary of Llandow Lodge, Llandow. 1500 yard.

24a *Footpath* Commences at the parish boundary east of Picket Farm and proceeds northwards crossing Footpath 24. Continues across fields and the railway to the parish boundary south of Parcau Farm. 1100 yards.

25. *Footpath* Commences on a roadway at the Parish boundary (South of Llampha Court) and near the remains of old chapel and proceeds southwest across fields and under railway bridge to the County road north of Clemenstone Lodge. Branch path from railway bridge eastwards across fields, turns northwards at a footbridge spanning stream and continues past Ysgubor-y-Parcau and across fields to the Parish boundary. 2400 yards.

26. *Bridleway* Commences at Heol-y-Slough at the junction of Footpath 5 and proceeds in a general north-westerly direction (crossing

Bridleroads 19 and 3) along the Western edge of Ogmore Down to terminate on the County road above Portobello House on the banks of the River Ogmore. 1700 yards.

27. *Bridleway* Commencing on the County road, southeast of Norton Hall, and proceeds along Pant Norton to the junction of Bridleway 26 on Ogmore Down. 600 yards.

28. *Cart road* Commences at the end of the County road north of St. Brides Church, St. Brides Major, and proceeds northwest to junction with Bridleways 2 and 29, on Ogmore Down. Continues westward across the Down past Southerndown reservoir to its junction with Bridleway 19 (Branch path turning northwest at a point east of the reservoir, crossing Ogmore Down to junction with Bridleway 19). 1700 yards.

29. *Bridleway* Commences at the junction of Bridleways 2 and 28 and proceeds northwest across Ogmore Down to the junction of Bridleways 19 and 21. 550 yards.

30. *Bridleway* Commences at the end of County road near Belmont, and proceeds northwest across Ogmore Down crossing Bridleways 2 and 21 to junction of Bridleway 19. 700 yards.

31. *Bridleway* Commences on the main road at Ogmore, near the junction of Heol-y-Milwyr, and proceeds southeast to junction with Bridleway 19 on Ogmore Down. 200 yards.

32. *Bridleway* Commences on Heol-y-Milwr, opposite Bridleway 20, and proceeds eastwards to junction with Bridleway 2 at the top of the Rhiw. 160 yards.

33. *Bridleway* Commences on the County road near Croes Antoni and proceeds northeast to junction with Bridleway 13 south of Brynawel. 220 yards.

34. *Footpath* Commences on the beach, midway between Cwm Mawr and Whitmore stairs and proceed eastwards along Cwm Bach following the course of the stream (Nant Cwm Bach) to the parish boundary. 700 yards.

35. *Footpath* Commences on the beach, below Whitmore Stairs, and proceeds to the cliff top where it turns southeast to the parish boundary. 260 yards.

36. *Bridleway* Commences on Bridleway 19 on Ogmore Down, and proceeds northeast across the Down, crossing Bridleway 2 (Heol-y-Milwyr) to junction of Bridleway 23, south of Flemings Down. 800 yards.

37. *Bridleway* Commences on the County road at the junction of Pant St. Brides and proceeds southeast across a field to the junction of Bridleway 33 near Croes Antoni. 100 yards.

38. *Footpath* Commences on the County road at Slon, Ogmore, and proceeds in a general northerly direction across a common and along the cliff-top turning inland near Bwlch Bach, to terminate on the County road north of Sutton. 1500 yards.

39. *Footpath* Commences on the County road near West Farm, Southerndown, and proceeds southeast along the cliff-top turning northeast and crossing Bridleway 40 to rejoin the County road at Little West House. 300 yards.

40. *Bridleway* Commences on the County road below Little West House and proceeds southeast (crossing footpath 39) along cliff headland to terminate on the County road leading to Southerndown Beach. 850 yards.

41. *Driftway* Commences on the County road near Pont-y-Brown and proceeds north along the eastern edge of Coed-y-Bwl turning northwest across downs to junction of Bridleway 13. 900 yards.

42. *Footpath* Commences at Sealand Farm proceeds along the wooded edge of the Cwm to the Keepers Lodge at Cwm Mawr, turning northward across Dunraven Park, through the Sea Walks of Dunraven and down on to Temple Shore. *Closed on November 11th, 1935.*

Daffodil Wood at Coed-y-Bwl

There are many daffodil strains competing for the right to be known as the Welsh National Flower, the wild daffodil—or Lent Lily—probably has the best claim of all.

One of the few remaining strains of wild daffodil still growing free in Britain is on the six acre Coed-y-Bwl Nature Reserve in Castle-upon-Alun, managed by the Glamorgan Naturalists Trust. This Nature Reserve was one of eighteen recipients of the 1975 Prince of Wales Award. The Prince of Wales established his Award for particular contributors to the Welsh environment in the 1970 European Conservation Year.

The Coed-y-Bwl Nature Reserve was established as a Glamorgan Naturalist Trust Reserve in 1971 and was formerly part of the Merthyr Mawr Estate. The original flowers were planted in the early 19th century by Mrs Nicholl of Merthyr Mawr. The flowers were known locally as 'Twm Dilies'.

The daffodils gradually became the target of a lot of picking and so it was leased from the Estate as a Reserve. It is six acres in extent, lying on limestone, which forms a valley side dropping away steeply to the River Alun. The wood is a delightful piece of preserved natural landscape, one mile east of St. Brides Major, and is the only daffodil wood in Glamorgan, the flowers numbering about a quarter of a million.

The Prince of Wales Award committee drew special attention in its citation to the management schemes developed by the Glamorgan Naturalist Trust to preserve the rare Lent Lillies. Whereas in earlier years the flowers were picked excessively and the woodland habitat trampled, the Trust has now constructed unobstrusive circular paths and invite visitors to enjoy the daffodils *in situ*. This action supported by the appointment of honorary wardens and the publication of a leaflet has provided a spectacle much appreciated by those who know the attractive Alun Valley.

The Prince of Wales Award—a triangular plaque—was presented by Prince Charles himself at a special ceremony in Monmouth in July, 1975. This plaque to be mounted permanently in a section of the stone wall surrounding the Coed-y-Bwl Reserve.

Countryside Treasures
within the Parish Boundary of St. Brides Major

Natural Reserves: Rare plants and grasses in Nature Reserve at Rhiw Forgan near Pan Quarry on Ogmore Down.
Wild Daffodils at Coed-y-Bwl, Castle-upon-Alun.

Geological: Geological phenomena, Carboniferous limestone rock formation at Twyn-y-Witch, Dunraven Bay, Southerndown.
A subterranean crevice running through the village of St. Brides Major, and known locally as Afon Dawal (Silent River). Caves under the cliffs at Southerndown leading to an air vent on the Common above called Twyll-y-Gwynt (Wind Hole).

Physiographical Ecological: Sand pits in Pant Marie Flanders on Ogmore Common.
Woodland Glades, the Alun river and rock faces at Pont-y-Brown, including an ancient stone slab footbridge, stepping stones and Ford at Stepsau Ddion under Castle-upon-Alun.

Ancient Monuments: Preserved ruins of Ogmore Castle and Stepping Stones over the Ewenny river. The Parish Church, and old Preaching Cross in the Churchyard, and the old stone Font of Croes Anthony overlooking the Church.

Roman Remains: The Old Roman road over the Ogmore Common, Heol-y-Milwr, (Military Road) and known locally as Pilgrims' Way.

Primitive Mine Works: Old diggins of lead mines and ancient Burial Place on Ogmore Down. The old Sutton stone quarries at Ogmore-by-Sea. Stone from these quarries was used in the Houses of Parliament at Westminster and the Vatican City in Rome.

Pools and Ponds: Pitcot Pool in St. Brides Major and The Dewpond (Pwyll-y-Mere) on the Cymdda at Southerndown.

Scenic Points of Vantage: From Heol-y-milwr on Ogmore Down giving a commanding view of exceptional beauty covering the district Gower coast to the West. The Swansea Bay and the Bwlch (Gateway to the Rhondda) to the North. The Caerphilly mountains to the East. The villages of the Vale of Glamorgan, the Bristol Channel and the Somerset and Devon coastline to the South.

Stone Work: Semi-dry stone walls peculiar to this part of the Vale of Glamorgan. A good example of this work may be seen on the roadside near Little West Farm at Southerndown. Another type of stonework known as Snail Creep may be seen on Dunraven Lodge at Seamouth, Southerndown, on Tusker House, Ogmore-by-Sea and the Ogmore Mill Farm, Ogmore.

Stone Wells: Adam's Well, near Ogmore Castle. Pant Mari Flanders. Jacob's Well under Castle-upon-Alun. Fynnon Dewi on the cliff edge in Southerndown. Ruth's Well near Stepsau Ddion and Pitcot Well.

Outstanding Phenomena: The sunsets at Ogmore-by-Sea are claimed to be the finest in the principality, giving name to a small Bay Ffynnon Orens (Orange Fountain).

Rights of Way: Public rights of way include Bridleways, Footways and Driftways, numbering forty two in all.

Winter Sport: Tobogganing down the Slip on the common in the Pant, and skating on Pitcot Pool.

Pony Trekking: Over the numerous Bridleways over Ogmore Down and Old Castle Down.

Stone Walling

Throughout the parish are some fine stone walls dividing fields and bordering roadways and commons. These walls are worthy of mention because of their method of construction, combining economy with strength.

Their foundations were built in lime mortar upon which was built about eighteen inches of dry walling, then another twenty four inches of mortared walling followed by another portion of dry walling, finishing with a 'string' course, and topped by a rough Scotch Coping. The object of the projecting 'string' course is to prevent trespass by sheep which graze on the common. It is well known that sheep will not attempt to climb a projecting overhang.

To provide mortar for these walls was very expensive, coal being particularly costly, so timber was used extensively to burn lime from the lias stone. This is the reason why lime kilns were built either near the sea shore where there is an abundance of washed up timber, or inland near a wooded area.

The remains of some of these kilns can still be seen dotted around the countryside. There is one on the Common on the sea front under Craig-yr-eos and a double one near Blackhall, St. Brides Major.

A fine example of these particular stone walls can be seen near Littlewest Farm, Southerndown.

Village History

It was the usual thing on Sunday mornings to see a number of carriages parked outside the parish Church, while their owners were at divine service. The horses drawing these carriages were stabled at the Greyhound Inn (now a private dwelling), where, behind locked doors the coachmen and grooms, with their top hats and cockades, would be partaking of the local brew (from Broughton Brewery). Afterwards they would chew parsley, so that their employers would not detect the smell.

There was always a plentiful supply of parsley in the Greyhound garden as it was grown specially for this purpose.

The Pound

At the lower part of the village was a stone-built compound known as the Pound (Yr Gorlan). In the old days this was used extensively as any animals caught straying in the village were put into the Pound and would only be released upon payment by the owner.

Many cottagers owned donkeys, which for some was their only means of transport, to bring home the harvested fern from the common to use as bedding for pigs and to provide manure for the garden. It was quite natural therefore, that these animals were the biggest offenders. I well remember seeing as many as six donkeys at one time in captivity, awaiting their owners.

Ogmore Down Burial Ground

We wondered what story surrounded the human bones found by workmen while excavating a trench near the Fox and Hounds Inn, for the new sewerage scheme. It was thought that these bones were at least 500 to 1000 years old. Was it a link with the early iron age cemeteries?

It is said that such a cemetery existed on Ogmore Down, near the old Roman road, or Pilgrims' Way, where in 1818, two remarkable helmets ornamented with enamel were found. These, unfortunately, were lost on the way to London by stage coach.

Nearby can be seen traces of old diggings, but these are in no way connected with the above. My father told me that lead was mined on this part of the common, but the output failed to compensate for the cost of transport and the project was discontinued.

Close by was a cairn of stones marking the spot where the son of Groes Farm, together with his horse, was struck by lightning and killed. He was returning from Bridgend via Rhiw Forgan over the Down. This cairn of stones was removed when extensive stone quarrying took place.

Castle-upon-Alun

Castle-upon-Alun lies about one and a quarter miles due east of the village of St. Brides Major, over looking the river Alun.

Apparently nothing is known of this Castle, but it is thought that the Castle which once stood on this historic site could have been a Welsh Castle of pre Norman times.

It has now been established that Castle-upon-Alun Farm was once an old thatched farm house, entered from the road through a gate, up some stone steps to a lovely stone arched doorway. There are several stone arches in the vicinity, relics of the old original building. The access to the bedrooms was by a stone stairway in a dark corner of the kitchen. This farm could possibly have been the Home Farm of the old Castle.

At Castle-upon-Alun, workmen unearthed three graves of the first century Roman-Celtic period, containing iron spears and daggers.

Sham Fights

In the late 1890s and the early 1900s, The Glamorgan Volunteer Regiment, staged Sham Fights on Ogmore Down. These exercises took place at weekends and would last all day. The sound of rifle fire could be heard for miles around and I remember as a boy, searching the Down for empty cartridges to use as whistles. In November, 1976, the Southerndown Golf Club made a new No. 5 green in the valley opposite Pant-yr-Norton. During the excavations two empty .303 rifle cartridge cases were

2nd VOLUNTEER BATTALION, WELCH REGIMENT, 1910.
Local members who took part in 'Sham Fights' on Ogmore Down.
Back Row: T. David, I. Thomas, L. Ace, E. Williams, T. Hopkin, A. Benjamin, T. Ace.
Seated: R. Lloyd, T. Dixon, G. Lloyd, J. Ace, E. Hardee.

found. Mr Anthony Jury a groundsman working on this construction immediately recognised them, and, being a local inhabitant, remembered the sham fights. He collected them and handed them to me. They were in a good state of preservation. They are another link with the past.

Sutton Stone

Sutton stone is claimed to be the only stone of its kind which when taken from the quarry can be sawn. The stone used in the area was sawn at the sawmill at Merthyr Mawr, and large blocks of the stone can be seen lying in the wood around the Mill. Unlike other stone which deteriorates by time and weather, Sutton stone hardens in the elements.

Sutton stone is a vein running through the local lias stone and out-cropping at 'Corner Ddu' in Southerndown Bay and on the beach at Wick.

The Sutton stone work in the Parish Church and the old village School testify to the quality and craftsmanship of local stone masons. The windows of the old School were the latest where stone from Sutton Quarries was used for building purposes. The quoins, mullions and cills were rebated to take glass without the use of wood. These windows were the work of Alexander Bevan of Pool Cottage, St. Brides Major—my grandfather.

The pulpit and Font in the Parish Church are also of Sutton stone and close examination will show that numerous small holes have been artificially filled. The reason why the stone was not favoured by monumental masons was that when facing the stone for inscribing they would discover a small shell or fossilization which would mean cutting another face or filling the hole artificially.

Gwilym and Richard Twrch both worked in Sutton Quarries, they were brought up by a retired Monk called Crallo ap Gruffyn. 'Old Crallo' who had been forcibly retired at the Dissolution, lived in a small cottage on the banks of the Ogmore river. Gwilym and Richard met and fell in love with the same girl and quarrelled so bitterly over her that neither spoke to the other again. Gwilym departed for Italy and remained there for about twenty years, later returning to Glamorgan an authority on Grecian and Italian styles of architecture. Gwilym Twrch was the architect and sculptor of the beautiful work of the porch of Beaupre Castle near Cowbridge completed about 1600.

Local Transport

Mr Thomas Rowe of Southerndown Farm, ran the first passenger service by horse brake between Southerndown and Bridgend. This vehicle was open with a canvas canopy and when travelling through the village he would herald his approach by blowing shrill blasts on a whistle. At the end of the First World War his son, of Fashoda House, started a taxi service from Southerndown to Bridgend with one vehicle only. Later he acquired a charabanc to seat thirty persons. This was a great advancement in local transport.

Mr John Thomas, the local undertaker, carpenter and wheelwright, started a taxi service from St. Brides Major to Bridgend, starting with a six seater Daimler and later with two Model T Ford cars. This service was successful and continued for several years and was then handed over to a relative, Mr Walter Berrett of Green Gate, St. Brides Major, who called the service 'The Reliance'.

Mr Berrett's brother was Chief Detective Inspector James Berrett and was one of the 'Big Five' of Scotland Yard, and the only detective with a beard in London. He was the officer who arrested Kennedy and Brown for the callous murder of Police Constable Gutteridge in London.

Later Mr Harry Gosling of Broughton, started a regular bus service between Llantwit Major and Bridgend, called the 'Vale Bus Service', later the name was changed to 'The Green and White Motors'. This service was well patronised because you only had to stand at your gate to be picked up and then on the return journey you could be put down where ever you requested. In the 1930's the Green and White Motors was taken over by the Western Welsh Omnibus Company.

Village Shows

It was a great occasion for the young people when the shows came to the village. Wonderful coloured placards would be posted up in the village, a week ahead, announcing the forthcoming attractions. This gave the parents of the children, the opportunity to get extra chores done for a few extra pence to spend at the shows. I well remember being given the job of picking potatoes for my father and promised some extra coppers to spend at the shows, which was on the village green opposite our house. Hearing the sound of the show organ, I could'nt get the job done quickly enough, so using childlike ingenuity, I took the shovel and covered over the remaining unpicked potatoes, little realising that next year my little scheme would come to light, which it eventually did, in the spring.

After the show had gone, I remember taking the horse Picton to the field and practising riding bareback, trying to copy a bareback riding stunt I had seen in the show. After much practice I found I could jump on and off at the gallop, but on one of these leaps I failed to come off and I swung around the horse's neck, locking my feet to prevent myself from falling. My jacket, however, being unbuttoned hung loosely down to the floor and was stepped on by the horse, with the result that it tore off under the armpits. Disillusioned I returned home prepared for the wrath of my mother, carrying the torn part in my hand and wearing a greatly diminished jacket.

Another occasion in the village was the periodical visit of the cheap-jacks or china-sellers. Offering their wares, from eggcups to chamber pots, they would set up their stands on the forecourt of the Greyhound Inn. When darkness fell the stalls would be illuminated by paraffin flares, which emited clouds of dense smoke. These sales were of great benefit to the parishioners because it must be remembered that the nearest shops were in Bridgend and this meant walking the distance and carrying home any goods purchased.

Very few tradesmen called from outside the village. An exception being Jones the Flannel who would visit once a month with his one-horse

The Farmers' Arms and Pitcot Green.

van, carrying rolls of Welsh flannel etc. Also a Mr Tucker of Cowbridge would call once a week. His wares consisted of fish, fruit and paraffin all on the same cart. If you could catch him in a good mood coming out of the Farmers' Arms, you could bank on him giving you a banana or an apple.

Cottages

Situated on Penylan Road about one hundred yards south of the Methodist Chapel, is a double-fronted house called Crofta. This house was once a blacksmiths shop and also a police station. It was in the large croft attached to the house overlooking the village that the people in the district gathered for the last time, before emigrating to Salt Lake City to join Brigham Young in the Mormon faith. It is said that the work of the Mormon missionaries was so successful that the population of St. Brides Major was depleted and to this day people from America, the descendants of those emigrants, keep visiting the district.

Across Pitcot Green opposite the Farmers' Arms, were two semi-detached thatched cottages. It was in one of these cottages, in 1863, that the Baptist Faith was founded in the parish, by a woman with the name of Peggy Saunders. Later the present Baptist Chapel was built in the centre of the village on a site given by Mr Evan Smith of Great House, Southerndown. This plot of ground was copyhold, but later became freehold.

FOX & HOUNDS INN, 1910.
Daughters of the house, Myfanwy, Mabel, Edith, Lily and dog Bruce.

Nearby were two more thatched cottages and it was in one of these that George Francis lived. He didn't forget St. Brides School when he made his fortune in America.

There are only two thatched cottages left in the parish. One is the Star Cottage adjacent to Ogmore Castle and it has played a major part in the history of the parish. The other is Seamouth Cottage at Dunraven. This picturesque cottage has been for generations the home of employees of the Dunraven Estate and a mecca for artists. It is occupied and well preserved.

Adjacent to the Fox and Hounds is a stone built cottage, called Myrtle Cottage, once occupied by the Powell family and during the change of occupation, a tragedy occurred. While Mr Powell was loading the last load of his possessions the horse took fright and bolted. Mr Powell fell under the wheel of the waggon and was killed. St. Brides being such a close community, the accident cast a gloom over the whole of the parish.

In the early days the Fox and Hounds Inn brewed its own ale and to this day hop vines can be seen on the high wall bank of Brynhyfryd House behind the Inn. This cottage was once occupied by the Dixon, and later, the Pearce families.

'Bull Hill'—this peculiar name can be found on the Ordnance Survey Map and is at the road junction to Southerndown near the old Vicarage. The name was derived from a tragic accident which occurred at this spot, in which a farm labourer was crushed against a gate by a bull and killed. A cottage nearby is called Bull Hill cottage and was once the village Post Office, it is now occupied by Miss Grace Bevan the daughter of the late Lorenzo Bevan, the village blacksmith. Prior to the Post Office being at Bull Hill it was in a cottage in The Pant.

In the cottage next to the Pelican Inn, Ogmore, lived the Herniman family. There was Nick, Jim and Mary together with Mr and Mrs Herniman. Mary was an ardent worshipper and regularly walked across Ogmore Down to the Parish Church. She wore a huge black hat and was a well known figure in the Parish. Nick was a farm labourer at Ton Farm, Merthyr Mawr. He was a man of huge proportions while brother Jim was the opposite, of slight build and not too strong. He was employed by the Booker family of Slon as an 'oddman'. Later in life Nick, in spite of his strength, was taken ill and brought home to the cottage where he was put to bed in a downstairs room. While working on the farm Nick had a dog which was his constant companion and it came to the cottage with Nick and stayed alongside his bed. When Nick died the dog would not allow anyone to enter the room. Every kind of ruse was tried by the vicar, the undertaker, and the family, without success in removing the dog and eventually Mr William Rees of Ogmore Farm was called in and the dog was shot. 'Faithful to the end.'

The Heddin family lived in Penylan Cottage on Penylan Road. The father was a Police Sergeant in St. Brides Major. A daughter Mary was housemaid and stillroom maid at Dunraven Castle. She was well acquainted with the Dunraven family, in their London house in Park Lane, London, and Adare Manor, County Limerick, Ireland, at the time when footmen were powdered and wigged. In 1897, Mary married John Leyshon, of Aberavon, and came to live in St. Brides Major. Her brother Richard (Dick) also worked at Dunraven, after being a footman to the Earl of Shrewsbury. He lived in St. Brides Major, until he died and was buried in the Churchyard.

Ogmore Cottage adjacent to the Pelican Inn, Ogmore-by-Sea was the place where two Drake Shot of Cromwellian times were found. One embedded in the wall of the cottage and the other embedded in a tree in the garden. They were thought to have been fired during a siege by Cromwell of Ogmore Castle. This Shot is in the safe keeping of Mrs Olive Gwyn who lived at the cottage.

41

It is said that Madam Patti once sang in Ogmore Cottage. While she was staying at Waterton Hall, Bridgend, she visited Candleston because she believed that the sea air mingled with the scent of the pines was beneficial to her vocal chords. It was during one of these visits that she sang to friends in the cottage.

Oldest Inhabitant

It was to Castle-upon-Alun farm that John Ricketts and his family came from Shepton Mallet and settled in Wales. Job their eldest son, now 98 years old, is the oldest inhabitant in the parish and lives in a house bordering on Ogmore Down.

The Ricketts family moved from Castle-upon-Alun to a cottage in the village called Crofta, so called because of its large croft. It was here that John Ricketts worked at his trade as a wheelwright and carpenter, and Job remembers his father, assisted by his mother, fitting an iron band or tyre to the wheel of a cart. He also remembers, as a little lad, sitting on an upturned box watching a signwriter from Bridgend painting the name Bowen of Wallace, on a farm box waggon. This same waggon, with the original paint on it, may be seen in the National Folk Museum at St. Fagans.

While the family were living at Crofta, John Ricketts worked for Henry Phillips, coachbuilders, Derwen Road, Bridgend, now the Mid Glamorgan Motors. He walked to work every day, there being no other means of transport. The whole family of father, mother, four boys and three girls, moved to Bramerton House.

When the Vale of Glamorgan railway between Barry and Bridgend was built, Job, as a young lad, obtained a job as a powder monkey, carrying blasting material to the men working in the cuttings. He later obtained work, wheeling slag on a tip between Cefn and Kenfig Hill. He then started as a cleaner in the railway sheds at Barry and after passing a medical examination he served his apprenticeship and became a fireman and was stationed for a time at Hafod in the Rhondda, working on the coal trains running to the docks in Barry.

Job married a Miss Harding of Bridgend, settled down in St. Brides and had a family of four boys and one girl. To augment his earnings he took an allotment on the Ogmore Common where he reared horses and sheep. While working on the fence of his allotment, he was struck in the eye by a piece of strand wire, this so impaired his sight, that he was demoted from a first class driver to second class, with a reduction in wages.

The Vale of Glamorgan Railway was built by a company of mine owners, to link the collieries north of Bridgend with Barry.

Upon his retirement Job kept his allotment, and as a hobby took up the making of herbal medicine and is now known throughout the principality, for his herbal cures. He scoured the local woodland and common, collecting plants, flowers and grasses. Strong sounding names like mountain flax, shepherd's purse, and peppermint plant, are used to serve up a herbal tea and bring relief to numerous complaints. 'I have great faith in herbs and don't bother much with doctors,' says Job.

Parish Characters

William Yorath, affectionately known as Billy, was born in Tyn-y-caeau Farm. He was the Parish Church organist for forty years and carried out his mother's wishes by playing the church organ at her funeral. Billy was always in great demand throughout the parish to play at parties, dances and for charity organisations with his own little dance band. His father was a relief organist in the Church and his grandfather, Mr Llewellyn Yorath, was a member of the School Attendance Committee, in 1876.

William Jenkins, a native of Wick, used to travel to Bridgend two or three times a week on his donkey and cart. On his way home it was his custom to stop at the Farmers' Arms for his usual couple of pints. He would tether his donkey to the field gate alongside the inn, (now the inn car park). Across the village green is Pool Farm, then farmed by Thomas Hardee, who had four sons and two daughters. Two of these boys seeing the donkey tethered in the usual place, decided to play a joke on William. They crossed the green, taking care not to be seen, took the donkey into the field, closed the gate, pushed the shafts of the cart through the gate and harnessed the donkey back between the shafts—and hid to watch the results. When William came out of the inn and saw the donkey on one side of the gate and the cart on the other, he didn't know what to do. He called for help and swore he would never touch another drop in his life. He thought he had either suffered a stroke or was seeing things!

There was another character who lived in Heolymynydd by the name of Richard Williams, known locally as 'Dick-a-Billy'. He was a little man and was proud of his long flowing white beard. He would walk down through the Pant Marie Flanders to the Portobello Hotel, where for a pint of beer as a wager, he would lift a prostrate man up from the floor with his beard. After winning his wager he would go on to the Pelican Inn and repeat his act.

On the Fox and Hounds lane is a little one roomed stone built building with a chimney and one window. In my young days this was where John Tait lived. A native of Scotland, he was a quiet and inoffensive man, respected and well liked. He earned a meagre living by mole and rabbit catching on the surrounding farms. Everybody passing his open door on the way to the bakehouse would stop for a chat with old John. The children were fascinated by his Scottish accent. My mother being Scottish always enjoyed a chat about Scotland and one day he confided in her and told her that he had once been caught in Scotland for salmon poaching.

Blacksmith

In the middle of the village on the main road, next to the Post Office stores, is a stone-built ground floor building (now a stores). It was the blacksmith's shop, run by the Bevan family. The last person to occupy the forge was Thomas Bevan.

Here all the horses and donkeys, from a wide area were brought for shoeing. The children on their way to school would stand in the doorway to watch the smithy, Lorenzo, fashioning a shoe from the white hot and sparkling iron and working the huge bellows, the handle of which was capped with a polished cows horn. I still remember the song Lorezno used to sing, it was 'Goodbye my bluebell, farewell to you', keeping in time with the bellows. Once a very obstinate donkey was brought to the smithy to be shod and when approached, kicked out in all directions. Several attempts at shoeing failed and in desperation and not wishing to be beaten by a donkey, Lorenzo put his huge arms around the donkey's body and lifted it off the ground, and let the animal kick against the wall, until it became exhausted. He then put it down on its feet and finished the job.

A favourite game among the boys and girls, at that time, was bowling a hoop with a crook, the crook was often fashioned from the handle of a galvanised bucket. Whenever a boy or girl could obtain a length of ¼ in. or ⅜ in. iron rod, they would take it to the blacksmith who, for a few coppers would fashion it into a hoop. I am afraid many iron hurdles in the farm fields disappeared.

A familiar sight too, was the banding of a wheel. The wheel of a cart or waggon, made by the local wheelwright, was clamped down on a huge heavy iron disc, outside the forge. The correct measurement was made with a revolving hand disc. The band or tyre was heated all round to a cherry red, carried out with special tongs and driven over the wooden wheel. It was immediately cooled with water, thus causing the metal to contract, making a tight and secure fit.

Stone Mason

George, the brother of Lorenzo Bevan the village blacksmith was a notorious character and a wonderful stone mason. He was once working for a contractor on a building as a 'banker' hand. This is a skilled part of a mason's work which means dressing stone before being put in the building. Now George was a tall man and complained of an aching back but the foreman refused him the use of a bench on which to work on the stone. His repeated requests fell on deaf ears. So George, when the foreman was absent, dug a hole in the ground in which to stand and so relieved the pain in his back. No-one in the area could build a dry wall like George Bevan, but he had one failing . . . he 'Tippled'. One day returning from the Fox and Hounds 'as full as an egg', George met the local vicar. The conversation went like this;

Rev. Jones, 'George! tch! tch! Drunk again?'

George, 'Yes sir, so am I.'

This story has been handed down first repeated by the vicar himself who had quite a sense of humour.

The Cobbler

A cottage in the Pant near the chestnut trees (now modernised) was the village shoemaker's shop. The shoemaker was William John, who lived with his brother Thomas, they were both bachelors and cooked and fended for themselves. William, known affectionately as Bill John the Cobbler, was a wonderful craftsman and could make you a pair of shoes from the 'bends' of leather stacked in his workshop. Bill knew every man, woman and child in the village and everybody knew Bill John. The only time you could see Bill without his leather apron on, was when he would walk up through the village on a Sunday, to worship at Horeb Baptist Chapel.

We children were always willing to go on an errand to the cobblers, because we were always sure of an apple from his orchard. We loved to see the cuckoo clock and would often wait an hour to see the cuckoo appear through the little door.

Periodically Bill John would walk around the village delivering his bills and collecting the money for work done. This is how some of the bills were worded.

Soleing and heeling Thommy	3/6 pence
Tipping toe and heel John	9 pence
Stitching wife and Maggie	1/6 pence
Nailing Willie	9 pence
Hob nailing Evan	1/3 pence

All this in lovely copperplate writing.

Village Bakery

In many houses in the parish there were brick-built ovens where the cottagers baked their own bread and cakes. These ovens were heated with drift wood gathered on the shore at Dunraven Bay. The fire was lit inside the oven and kept going until the internal brickwork was practically red hot. The red embers would then be withdrawn and the oven cleaned of all ashes and dust. The waiting loaves were then placed on the oven bottom and the door closed. This was a weekly undertaking. Later a village bakehouse was built, and this proved a success as it was found more convenient and labour saving. On the Thursday prior to the baking the children would be sent to the bakehouse for yeast and as the baker's name was Mr West it was thought a huge joke to say, 'please Mr West for a pennyworth of yeast'. Friday was the day for communal baking and the children would take their mother's loaves of bread and cake to the bakehouse on their way to school at dinner time and collect them after school. When the tins were filled with dough they were placed on the table waiting for the baker to put them into the oven, each had been marked with a slip of paper bearing the owner's name. The children would walk around them and, if there was someone they didn't like, they would dig their finger into the dough and run.

After school the children would go to collect their loaves and it was amusing to see the different means of transport employed. Prams, trollies, clothes baskets and even wheelbarrows were used. If a tin had been overfilled it would overflow when baking and there was great competition among the children to be first to the bakehouse to receive from the baker this lovely golden crust.

Mr West was followed by Mr W. Cox and later by Mr Alex Bevan. The old bakehouse was situated on the Fox Lane and has now been converted into a dwelling house.

BRYN SION METHODIST CHAPEL
SUNDAY SCHOOL OUTING TO PORTHCAWL, 1936
Back Row: D. Thomas, E. Lloyd, W. Powell, B. Powell, M. Morgan, L. Howe, E. Harry, A. Morgan, G. Sharrat, E. Williams, M. Sneddon, N. Watkins, P. Whitfield, B. Blomley, E. Blomley, M. Smith, F. Morgan, P. Blomley. *Front Row:* I. Watkins, Rev. T. Watkins, W. Jenkins, E. Williams, M. Williams, G. Jenkins, D. Sneddon, J. Hopkin, M. Morgan, B. Glover.

Village Shop and Bryn Sion Chapel

During my young days the shop in St. Brides Major was kept by Mr Thomas Howe, a deacon in Bryn Sion Methodist Chapel. He was also the conductor of the Chapel Choir and was presented with a conductor's baton by the Choir. Mr Thomas Morgan, Penuchadre Farm, played the organ. In later years the organ has been played by Mrs Bronwen Jenkins and the violin by Mrs Blodwen Rees, who has played in the Chapel since her school days.

Village Shop

The village shop and Post Office, is situated in the centre of the village and is kept by David Evans and his wife Margaret. Mr Evans is a past President of the South Wales and Monmouthshire Grocers' Federation, and a member of the Bridgend and District Rotary Club.

The shop window has not always been full of groceries. During the Coronation, it was crammed full with a magnificent display of silver cups, won by the various organisations in the parish and was insured for £1,000. On Coronation Day itself, Mr and Mrs Evans decided to leave the shop for an hour, to watch the village tug-of-war competition. They were happy in the knowledge that the window was insured but when the local policeman saw them walk on the field, knowing what was in the shop window, he stopped tugging on the rope and ran all the way back to guard the shop.

The one and only telephone kiosk in the village was situated against the wall of the shop. It was while a local housewife was making a call to Bristol that a terrific bang occurred and the person to whom she was speaking said, 'What was that?' She received the answer, 'I think it was a car backfiring'. Little did she know, that the bang that was heard in Bristol, was the safe in the shop being blown up by burglars, during the absence of Mr and Mrs Evans. The burglars had covered the safe with bags of flour and it can be imagined the sight that greeted Mr Evans upon his return, to find the interior of his shop completely smothered in flour. It was not until the following day that the housewife realised how near she had been to the explosion. The burglars were never caught.

First Policeman

In December, 1839, it was decided at Quarter Sessions that a small 'trial' force of one Superintendent and six Constables should be formed to police the one part of the County in which the need for professional policeman was greatest. So successful was this experiment that, at the beginning of 1841, Quarter Sessions agreed that the small police force should be extended to cover the whole of the county. The authorised strength of this new Force was one Chief Constable, four District Superintendents, nine Sergeants and twenty-five Constables. The Force to be patterned on the Metropolitan Police, which had been introduced by Sir Robert Peel in 1829.

Robert Herniman of Ogmore Cottage, the great grandfather of Mrs Olive Gwynne of the same address, was a 'Peeler' before becoming the first Constable in St. Brides Major. At this time he would walk through Ewenny and Corntown to the Assizes in Cardiff. He wore the uniform of the Peelers, i.e. a pilot blue swallow-tail coat, with pockets inside the tail to accommodate staff, handcuffs and rattle, a leather collar (the stock) under the coat collar as a protection against attacks on the throat, blue trousers (white in summer) and the fashionable tall hat of the times.

After the First World War, two policemen, later reduced to one, were stationed at Southerndown. Now, with radio links, the parish is policed by car from Bridgend and Wick.

Monumental Mason and Village Postman

At one time the Three Golden Cups, Southerndown, was kept by Mr Alfred Davies, who was also a sculptor and a monumental mason and in the corner of the field opposite the Inn was his workyard, some of his work may still be seen in the Churchyard. His last work was the First World War memorial stone, the last piece of Sutton stone quarried from the old quarry at the bottom of Pant-y-Slade and erected in the parish Church.

Overhanging the sculptor's yard was a very old oak tree, which brought tragedy to the parish. One winter's afternoon a terrible storm blew in from the Atlantic, William Morgan a local resident, together with a little lad of tender age was sheltering under the tree, but the wind was of such force that it uprooted the tree, bringing the wall alongside it down on top of the little lad and killed him. William Morgan received a crushed foot which crippled him for the rest of his life.

About two hundred yards further up the road from the Three Golden Cups is Sea View, a stone built house with a Welsh slate roof and was the home of the Harry family, consisting of William Harry and his wife Margaret, their two daughters Elizabeth and Isabella, their three sons David, William, and Ollison. David, affectionately known as 'Curly', was from a lad to the time of his old age retirement, employed at Dunraven Castle, starting as a pantry boy and finishing with his wife as caretakers.

William was the mail carrier employed by the Postal Authority to convey the mail from Bridgend, via St. Brides Major, to Southerndown. His horse-drawn vehicle can only be described as a glorified box on wheels. It was painted a brilliant red with the driver perched on the top without any kind of shelter from the elements.

His brother Ollison was the Southerndown postman and his delivery round extended from Dunraven Castle to the river mouth, including Heolymynydd and Norton. In World War One I served with him in the 2/1 line Glamorgan Yeomanry, he was a good cricketer and played for Southerndown.

Skating

Pitcot pool at the top of the village was well known throughout the district for skating and the Parish produced some very fine skaters. During a hard winter when ice formed on the pool, the children would be prevented from throwing stones on the surface, to preserve it for the sport. If the Dunraven family were at the castle they, with other gentry from miles around, would gather for an ice carnival.

ST. BRIDES MAJOR AIR RIFLE CLUB, 1950.
Back Row: G. Yorath, R. John, D. Hopkin, S. Phillips, J. Jones, G. Ricketts, W. Lloyd, C. F. Morgan.
Seated: R. Pearce, E. Hopkin, Mrs J. Thomas (Landlady of Fox & Hounds Inn), H. Sharrat, W. Cox.

Fires would be lit on the bank around the pool and it was a wonderful sight to see figures gliding past in the firelight. Drinks of hot toddy would be brought down from the nearby Farmers' Arms Inn and served on trays to the gathering. Many were there not to skate but to take part in the festivities. In those days wooden skates were used. These were made with hard wood and a steel blade fitted underneath, screwed into the heel of the boot and secured with leather straps. It was wonderful when the all metal skates were introduced and were called skeletons. These were clamped on to the boot and were adjustable. My daughter and I were both skaters and have still got our skates but unfortunately for many reasons they have not been used for many years.

Rifle Shooting

In 1890, the first rifle range was established in Southerndown, on the sea side of the footpath from Beach Road to the County Road near Green Lane. It was on this range at the age of ten, that I received my first prize, which was a framed photograph presented to me by Mrs Booker of Slon, who was President of the club.

In 1915, the 2nd Volunteer Battalion of the Welch Regiment (Dad's Army) was formed and the Dunraven Estate erected an up to date rifle range in the Athletic Field. Evening matches took place, the targets being illuminated by an ingenious method of acetyline gas jets. This enabled the club to shoot postal matches throughout England and Wales. The principal range officers were Thomas Hadden, head forester for the Dunraven Estate and William David of Norton Farm, both these men competed at Bisley. Southerndown small bore rifle club was without doubt the best in the Principality, ten of the members took part regularly at Bisley. I am proud to have been a member of this club and of my many medals, including a gold medal and The Glamorgan County championship in 1930, on the service rifle range at Newton, Porthcawl.

The art of rifle shooting, although it is now done by air rifle, has existed in the parish since early 1900. It was taught by Mr Thomas Hopkin to schoolboys so young that the rifle had to be held up by a tripod. St. Brides Major has continued to maintain a high standard even up to the time of this writing, and hold the position of top of the Bridgend and District Air Rifle League.

Southerndown Golf Club

Quite a large portion of the Ogmore Down is taken up by the Southerndown Golf Club. It is of international standard and is reputed to be one of the driest and one of the finest photogenic courses in the Principality.

In 1924, Major Sullivan the secretary, and Jock Kinear the head greens' keeper, journeyed by Campbell's steamer to Ilfracombe, where a drifter had been chartered to convey them to Lundy Island, for the purpose of surveying the possibility of forming a golf course on the Island. Evidently this plan never materialised.

In 1905, an Artisan Club was formed and a silver Challenge Cup was given for competition by the Ogmore Commoners. When the Artisan club became defunct the cup was given to the Mother Club and named the Commoners' Cup and is still competed for today.

In May, 1966, Southerndown Golf Club became the focal point for an American film company, where a film in the series 'Shell's Wonderful World of Golf' was filmed in colour. The stroke play match was between David Thomas of Wales who completed the round in 72, and Bob Rosburg of the U.S.A. who finished in 70. Fifty of the club members acted as extras. The Martini Professional Golf Championships has been held several times at Southerndown.

ARTISAN PLAYERS OF SOUTHERNDOWN GOLF CLUB, 1908.
The Captain, Alfred Davies, of the Three Golden Cups holding the trophy—The Commoners Cup.
Back Row: H. O. Irvine (Parent Club Captain), Reg. Harry, Evan Williams, Leyshon Ace, R. Walker
(Club Professional);
Middle Row: Fred Davies, Eric Wheeler, Richard Heddin, Dan Crowley, Harry Pearce, William Hill;
Front Row: Jose Wheeler, Olison Harry, Alfred Davies (Capt.), Christie Davies, George Williams, James
Sim. (Reg. Harry and Evan Williams later became Golf Professionals.)

SOUTHERNDOWN CRICKET CLUB, 1924.
Back Row: E. Bevan, R. Pearce, E. Jones, G. Richards, S. W. Bevan, P. Mitchel, H. Bevan, F. Thomas,
W. Pearce; *Seated:* W. Jones, W. Green, O. Harry, F. Pratt, A. Rowe, Q. Lewis, E. Ellsbury.

SOUTHERNDOWN MISSION ROOM CONCERT PARTY
(Outside the 'Nest', Ogmore-by-Sea, 1925)

Back Row: Richard Pearce, Gwyn Bevan, Jim Symes, Felix Bamon, Fred Pratt; *Second Row:* Violet Jordan, Connie Bevan (now Mrs Loomes Penyfai Post Office), Annie MacDonald, Maggie David, Nellie Symes, Nancy Owen, Thelma Lewis. *Third Row:* Gladys Verity, Bertha Bevan, Tom Bamon (who formed the concert party), Rev. David Vaughan (lay reader at Southerndown Mission Church), Mrs Arthur Rowe, Alice Thomas. *Front Row:* Stirling Bamon, Dulcie Thomas (now Mrs Wilson, Jersey), Eileen Thomas, Eileen Bamon (now Mrs Percy Green of Penyfai) and Jack Owen.

The Nesters

The Nesters Concert Party was started in 1920 by Thomas Bamon who lived at The Nest Cafe, Ogmore-by-Sea. He gathered about him a group of young men with little to do in the evenings and formed the concert party which became one of the major attractions in the area, until 1935 when they disbanded. Mr Bamon, the possessor of a fine baritone voice, had belonged to a concert party called the Roosters in the First World War. The Nesters used to hire the old church hall in St. Brides Major and run concerts, sometimes three a week. They appeared at the Town Hall, Cowbridge, the old Lambert Hall in Bridgend (which used to be on the old stone bridge), the Cottage Homes and at Wick. How many people can remember Billy Parker, the comedian, and his partner Mary Yorath in 'Here we are again' or perhaps 'Meet me tonight in the Cowshed . . . ' or 'I do like to be beside the Seaside'? The Nesters bought spotlights from the old Capitol Theatre in Cardiff and borrowed palm trees from the conservatories at Dunraven Castle and painted their own scenery. Many can remember the 'Old Pig and Whistle' set at the back of the old church hall stage.

Glow-Worms

Glow-worms are not now common in the Vale of Glamorgan but prior to 1950 there were plenty to be seen after dark on both sides of the road and on the common also on each side of the valley near 'Rhiw Forgan' which is now a Naturalist Trust area, because of the rare grasses which are found there.

Between the two World Wars many young people from the village worked in Bridgend, travelling to and fro on bicycles. Nine times out of ten the wind would be against them on the way home which meant that they had to walk and push their bicycles between (what we called) the mountains.

It was then we saw the Glow-worms, like little beacons, shining brightly in the grass. We used to pick them up and decorate our hats and coats, but would always place them back on the common before entering the village. Unfortunately they are now no more, the extensive quarrying of rock, heavy blasting and the coating of stone dust blown over the common, has apparently exterminated them. I have searched many times for them but have failed to find any of our little friends. Will we ever see them again?

'Y Fari Lwyd'

An old custom, usually kept up in rural parts of South Wales, was the Fari Lwyd or Holy Mary. This effigy, which has been discribed in many old books, was made from the skull of a horse, the jawbone hinged to enable the man carrying it to snap the teeth together with a most frightening sound. The head and man would be dressed in a bright red and yellow robe, with ribbons and tassels hanging down. The party carrying out the old tradition, was composed of four Welsh speaking men, who knew the locality and the inhabitants and could sing the required ritual songs.

They would call at a house, knock loudly on the door and commence to sing the special verses, which required an answer in Welsh. Should the tenant fail to answer, they would demand that the door be opened and expect to be invited in and partake of refreshment, such as mead, beer and bakestone cake. If the tenant was able to answer the standard questions in a 'Hwyl', semi-sung manner, the party would bestow a greeting and bless the house, before retiring to the next house.

My father, being a fluent Welshman, was able to answer correctly, standing in the porch behind the locked front door. In writing this, I remember the fear upon hearing the voices outside. We clutched our mother's skirt because we children had heard of the dreadful things (untrue of course) that 'Y Fari Lwyd' could do to us. At the end of the performance we would run upstairs to see them departing, looking out through the safety of the window. It is an old custom which has long since ceased to be carried out in this area.

Quoits

Up to the early 1900, the game of field quoits was a much favoured sport in the rural villages, and inter-village tournaments were looked forward to with great interest, by the young and old alike. The game was played in the centre of a field, with a bed of clay formed inside a heavy wooden frame, in the centre of which was a strong iron peg, driven deep into the ground. The clay beds were at each end of the pitch, the player having to stand at the back of the bed, when making his throw. The scores were by measurement to the peg, maximum score being a ringer, which meant that the player had thrown his quoit on to the peg.

The quoits were of hardened steel, approximately 10 ins. diameter, 1½ ins. wide and ¾ ins. thick. Players took great pride in keeping their quoits highly polished. When a player took his stand to make his throw, he would hold a quoit in each hand and strike them together giving forth a bell-like sound, which would be heard in the village. The art in throwing was to land the quoit edge-on into the clay. Should a quoit land flat it would slide or bounce, this would not register a score. There was also a juvenile team and I remember playing on more than one occasion and was very proud of my quoits, which were much smaller, but every bit as well polished.

A somewhat similar game is still played, and is much favoured, by the Americans who, instead of using the polished steel quoits, use horse shoes.

The quoit field in St. Brides Major was at the end of the lane off Penylan Road.

Halloween

Halloween or Apple Ducking Night, as it was better known, was an occasion looked forward to by the children of the village when some of their pals were invited to take part in the various competitions.

As soon as the table had been cleared of the tea things, washed and put away in the round wicker basket, much favoured in those days, the hanging oil lamp would be lit. The fire made up, giving the room a warm and exciting atmosphere, to await the friends.

A number of cords, which varied to the number of children taking part, would then be secured to the ceiling rafters. Tied on the end of each cord would be an apple covered with treacle. The contestant would wear an apron wrapped around the shoulders, to protect the clothes, and a cap or bonnet to protect the hair. The father would give the word 'GO' and the winner would be the first to bite away enough of the apple to free it from the string, without taking the hands from behind the back. The winner would then be presented with a prize, generally some sweets. A bowl of warm water and a flannel would then be used to remove the sticky treacle from the face and hair.

To continue the fun the family galvanised bath would be brought in and placed in the centre of the kitchen floor and filled two thirds with water. Some of the more considerate parents would add some hot water from the large cast iron kettle. Into this water would be thrown about a dozen apples. The contestants would then have their hands tied behind their backs, lean over the bath and endeavour to pick up an apple with their teeth. The father would have his watch on the table and time the contestants, the one who could pick out an apple in the shortest time would be declared the winner.

The mother would then see that all heads were thoroughly dry and after supper the friends would return home for bed and to discuss their evenings fun in school the next day.

Halloween was also the time for the young women to try to peep into the future and many of the love spells were tried, some in secret and others in the company of a girl friend.

In carrying out one of these a young single woman would put the white of an egg into a bowl of water taken from a well. When the water had settled, the egg white would portray the head of the man she would marry.

Another love spell practised in the neighbourhood was for the lovelorn lass, if she wished to read her future, she would take some garment—an undervest preferred as being worn next to the skin—to the nearest water, without the knowledge of any inmate of the house, and there soak it thoroughly. For the spell to be successful the garment should be carried in the teeth and hung over the back of a chair before a fire. The girl would retire to a distant part of the room and await the outcome. If the spell was properly carried out, the wraith of the girl's future husband should appear and, after turning the garment, would disappear as suddenly as he had appeared.

Another love spell was called the 'Knife' spell. Secrecy was again absolutely necessary. The maiden who wished to know her fate was required to place a knife in the corner of the leek bed in the garden. She had next to walk backwards around the leek bed, taking care not to stumble. If marriage was to be her lot, then the spirit of her future swain would appear and take the knife from the corner of the leek bed, replacing it in the sheath held by the girl. This would complete her happiness for she would subsequently marry. This last one is secretly carried out to this day. A maiden who received a portion of wedding cake would, upon retiring to bed, place it under her pillow when in her dreams she would see her future husband.

Poultry Keeping

A number of villagers, wherever it was possible, kept poultry, ducks, geese and chickens. When a hen grew past the laying stage, it was killed for the table. This was regarded as a treat and was usually kept for the Sunday dinner. The ducks and geese were reared and fattened and sold at Christmas.

When the geese showed signs of laying, a 'Tulk' was provided. This is a Welsh word meaning a shelter of a kind. It comprised two pieces of wood, slate or metal, about two feet square, placed on edge—the top edges brought together at the top and put against a wall or shed. Straw or hay was provided and the goose, assisted by the gander, would make a nest. As the eggs were laid they were brought indoors for safety from preditors. When the laying was completed the housewife would return the eggs to the nest and the goose would commence sitting. When it came time for hatching, the housewife would pay a daily visit to the nest and remove any gosling that had hatched and any broken pieces of shell to prevent injury. The newly hatched goslings were taken and put in a basket near the hearth to keep warm and taken out occasionally and given a drink of water and some very fine breadcrumbs.

Sometimes a hard shell would retard the hatching, the housewife would ascertain if the egg was addled or not by placing it in a bowl of luke warm water, if the egg rocked she would know that there was life inside and return the egg to the goose. Sometimes the goose would resent this interference and would strike out with beak and wing, which could cause quite severe bruising. When the hatching was complete and the brood returned to the goose they were then taken down to the pond and launched upon the water. It was indeed a pretty sight to see the goose, gander and the little ones swimming off in line astern.

When a goose was killed for Christmas care was taken to preserve the feathers which were carefully sorted out. A number of the large ones were tied together and fastened to a bamboo cane and used for dusting in high places, such as ceiling beams and tall furniture. The down feathers were selected and put into a large paper bag and then into a moderate oven, to dry out the natural oil, and these were then used to fill beds and pillows.

It took several years to collect enough feathers to fill a full sized bed. The wings of the goose was put under a flat stone and placed in the oven and dried. Very few dwellings were without a goose's wing which was used for dusting and proved very efficient especially with carved furniture. Goose wings are still favoured by Beekeepers for brushing the bees off the comb—the bees object to being removed by a brush but offer no objection to a goose wing. I have used this method as a beekeeper for nearly forty years.

The flake or fat of the goose was highly valued by the old people. It was rendered down and stored in a jar for medicinal purposes, throat trouble and especially quinsy.

Pig Killing

In my boyhood days the village was almost self supporting as every cottage had a garden and a pigsty. The cottager worked a rotation of crops to last the year. The custom was to purchase two young pigs, one to fatten and sell as a porker to a pork butcher, the other to kill and salt for the household.

There were two local men in the village who were proficient as pig slaughtermen, Mr Edward Hopkin and Mr George Atyeo.

It was a great event in the home when the time came for the pig to be killed. On that day the copper washing boiler would be lit to provide plenty of hot water. When this important ceremony took place the children would be sent on some pretext out of earshot, because, although they understood it was necessary, the unfortunate animal had become a pet and it was rather pathetic when the children were allowed to see the animal hanging from the special large hook in the ceiling in the back kitchen, after being dressed by the butcher. The carcase would be kept open for two days by a special spreader to dry and harden. The children were always interested when shown the black spots on the pigs front leg, supposed to be the marks left by the devil when he entered the swine and they ran into the sea, as mentioned in the scriptures.

Before the carcase was cut down the butcher would saw down on each side of the back bone. The back bone would then be cut into pieces about ten inches wide, these were called 'chines'. The rib bones were then lifted and the butcher would then ask the owner if he wanted large or small hams. The flitches and hams were now ready for salting. The fat, having been removed from the inside of the flitches, was rendered down into lard and stored in earthenware steens, the residue left from the rendering was much favoured and the children were often given some to go to school in lieu of sweets. These were known as 'crusons'.

When a pig was killed, there was often more fresh meat than the cottager required for his immediate use, so the gifts of a chine, sparerib, steak, etc., was made to the neigbours who, in turn, would made a similar gesture when they killed their pig.

The Farmers Feast

Every June a great event took place in the parish, this was the Farmers' Feast. For weeks ahead preparations were started for the event which was held in the long room of the Farmers' Arms Inn.

The women would attend a special service in the parish Church, after which they would walk up through the village to the Farmers' Arms, where they would be met by the men all dressed in their Sunday best clothes which varied according to their profession. Stone masons always wore a monkey jacket and white corduroy trousers, while carpenters wore a white collar and black tie.

The long room would be decorated with flowers and evergreens and the tables laden with all kinds of home-made cakes and sandwiches, pitchers of beer, cider, mead and home-made wines. When the meal was over, there was always enough food left over to supply the children who would be gathered on the village green, opposite the Inn, to watch and listen to the music. After the room had been cleared of chairs, tables and benches and the floor swept, a couple of tallow candles were shredded with a knife and scattered over the floor. The dance would commence by the Master of Ceremonies and his partner 'dancing the room' to open the 'Ball'. The music for dancing was provided by a three-piece orchestra consisting of a Harp, a Piccolo and a Violin. The harpist, who always on these occasions wore a black 'wide awake' hat, was Mr Pearce the well known Welsh harpist, who had been hired for this special occasion.

An old lady from Wick, known for her skill in making boiled sweets and brandy snaps, would attend the Farmers' Feast and sit on a bench under the veranda selling her wares in paper pokes.

Gleaning

The labour force in the parish, with the exception of those employed by the Dunraven Estate, was entirely agricultural. It was usual for cottagers not employed on the farm to give a helping hand with the hay and corn harvest and, in return, they would be allowed to plant a row of potatoes in the field alongside the farmers' potatoes, or if he had a large garden, he might prefer a load of manure.

At the end of the hay and corn gathering, the last load brought in from the field was an event all the children looked forward to and it was called harvest home. Often the last load would be a small one and the children would be allowed to ride on top and would sing all the way to the rickyard, where they would partake of tea and cakes provided by the farmer's wife; the men would be given beer or cider from an earthenware jar and horn beaker. The object of the stone jar and horn beaker was that it could be thrown up or down from the top of the waggon without fear of breakage.

There were many ways in which the farmer would help the cottagers, one being to allow them to go gleaning before he turned his geese out on-to the stubble. The wife, whose husband had been a helper, would take her children, all supplied with sacks, to the field where they would pick the heads of corn left behind by the farmers' rake. It was often a bonus if they found a sheaf which had been thrown into the hedge and forgotten. These bags would be brought home to the cottage where the family's galvanised bath would be placed in a convenient place in the garden. The mother and children would then sit around the bath, taking the corn heads one at a time and rubbing them hard between their hands they separated the seeds from the husks. When the bath was about half full it would be taken further away from the house and one of the children would then stir with a broomstick whilst another would apply the household bellows and blow out the chaff. The clean grain would then be poured into a sack, the bath returned and the process repeated. Often enough grain was collected in this way to supply the cottager's poultry for many months.

Sanding and Whitening

Nearly all the cottages in the parish had solid floors in the parlour, kitchen and back kitchen. It was the custom to clean these floors, which were composed of either mortared concrete, paving stones or brick blocks, by scrubbing and then sprinkling them with fine sand. Sand for this purpose could be purchased from a local character known to us children as 'Sando' because, when hawking the sand around the village, he would call 'Sando' in a very loud voice, often imitated by the children. In a house where there were many children he did very little business because the children would be sent to the sand pit in Pant-Marie Flanders, near Heolymynydd, where there was an unlimited supply. In Pant-Marie Flanders there is a lovely old stone well, on which at one time the people of Heolymynydd and Ogmore village were dependent for their drinking water; it was at this well that we as children used to drink when fetching the sand.

Another journey, which we as children were sent on, was to Broughton and down into Monkash Cwm, where we would dig alongside the brook for 'Marl'. This marl was widely used by the housewives for whitening the hearthstone and entrance doorstep. Some of the women took great pains to work a scalloped design along the out edge of the fireplace and front doorstep. Often the interior of the dwelling was judged by the lovely scalloped doorstep. There was an unofficial competition among the inhabitants as to who could produce the most artistic design.

A custom prevalent in the district was the white-washing of the interior and exterior of the dwelling houses and out-buildings to add to the cleanliness and picturesque appearance. Underneath there was a deeper meaning. The good people believed that this general whitening shut the door against the devil. Unslaked white lime could be obtained locally at little cost and was used extensively for agricultural purposes.

The Parish Church

The chancel part of the Church was built in the twelfth century by Simon de Londres while the other part was probably built in the thirteenth or fourteenth centuries. The church building itself is full of points of interest. Over the centuries it has become studded with monuments of various kinds installed in memory of past benefactors and patrons. On the side wall of the chancel hangs an incised stone rubbing of the famous Arnold Butler, dressed in the full regalia of a knight. This was taken off his coffin lid which is now lodged under the altar of the church.

On the north side of the Sanctuary is a monument in the shape of a canopied table tomb on which lie two effigies of a man in armour and a woman in period costume. It is believed to be the tomb of the Butlers as

The Parish Church of St. Bridget with the Church School and School House in background.

it bears the engravings of cups or goblets. (The family crest of the Butlers consists of three golden cups.)

In a small alcove separating the chancel and the nave stands the statuette of Bridget, the Patron Saint of the Church. She lived in the fifth century, the daughter of an Irish Chieftain who was famous for founding several religious communities and for brewing a special ale called 'Cwrw Ffraidd'.

In the Norman tower is a peal of six bells (formerly five) presented by the late Caroline, Countess of Dunraven. When one of the bells cracked they were sent, in 1938, to Loughborough for recasting into six. They are erected on modern bearings and new girder work and are reputed to be one of the most modern in Glamorgan. The beautiful stained glass windows are of more recent date.

The clock in the tower was dedicated on Sunday, November 9th, 1919, to the memory of those from the Parish who laid down their lives for their Country during the Great War, 1914-1918. Also in the church is a Sutton stone plaque in memory to the fallen of both World Wars, 1914-1918 and 1939-1945.

Painted on the wall over the archway leading into the chancel was a beautiful coloured scroll, bearing the words 'Holy, Holy, Holy, Lord God Almighty'. Over the doorway leading out into the porch was another scroll of a similar design with the words 'Remember Thy Creator

Inside the Church of St. Bridget showing the scrolls over the Chancel.

In The Days Of Thy Youth'. Unfortunately both of these lovely scrolls have been obliterated. St. Brides Major is fortunate that old photographs have shown these lovely scrolls before they were covered.

There are many churches throughout the Vale where discoveries have been made revealing some ancient scrolls and painting, and care has been taken to preserve these relics of the past.

In the Churchyard, which belongs to the Parish Council and not to the Church, stands an old stone built Preaching Cross, the top of which, like many of the crosses in the Vale, was destroyed by Cromwell. The steps of this cross are indented and worn—it is said by the Pilgrims kneeling in prayer. It is also believed that these indentations were caused by agricultural workers sharpening their sickles and knives before going out to the fields. By so doing they hoped to receive a divine blessing on their labour and be blessed with a bounteous harvest.

Southerndown Reading Room

The Southerndown Reading Room was a corrugated iron building with drop tables secured to the walls, and was opened on September 10th, 1876. To commemorate the opening little books were presented to the children of the parish by Miss Florence Lysaght of Newport, Monmouthshire. These little books had a picture cover and had stories from the Bible and were signed by Miss Lysaght, September 18th, 1876. Two of these books are still in the possession of Mrs Olive Gwynne of Ogmore Cottage. The Reading Room was eventually consecrated and became known as The Southerndown Mission Room. In 1967, under the Glamorgan County road widening scheme, the Mission Room was demolished together with the adjacent house known as Castle View. To replace the Mission Room a small modern church was built and is called All Saints, Southerndown.

The Church Hall

In the early part of 1919 the Vicar of the parish, the Rev. Frank Picton Warlow, thought it would be a splendid thing if the young people of the parish, who were returning to civilian life from the services, had somewhere to go to enjoy themselves in the evenings. A committee was formed and it was resolved that a collection be made throughout the parish. This was done and subscriptions were received from all denominations in the parish. Various functions were held in the village school to augment the fund and eventually a sectional building was purchased and erected on the site where the present Church Hall now stands and was called the Village Institute. The building being erected on 'Glebe' land, no cost of land purchase was incurred. The scheme was a huge success and in a short time the building was extended and an anti-room and canteen added.

All the functions of the parish, including dances, whist drives, concerts, public meetings, etc., were held in the Hall, which was non-political and non-sectarian. A full-sized billiards table was purchased from Dunraven Castle by Mr R. M. Dillwyn of Castle-upon-Alun and presented to the committee and was a wonderful addition. Many tournaments took place on this table.

After the death of the Rev. Picton Warlow, the Rev. J. Llew Croft became the Vicar of the parish and the Institute was run by a properly selected comittee, the secretary being John Bishop Hopkin of Littlewood, St. Brides Major. At an annual general committee meeting the Vicar took the chair and declared that, the building being on 'Glebe' land, he had had deeds drawn up and the building now belonged to the Church and it would thereafter be known as the Church Hall. Some years ago a new permanent building was erected on the same site and is in constant use.

St. Brides Major School

The first Church School in the Parish was adjacent to the Parish Church with only a stone wall separating it from the Churchyard. The first headmaster was Mr E. Hayden, a native of Belfast brought from Ireland in 1863 by the Dunraven family and installed as master. Mr Hayden had the reputation of being a strict master and an excellent teacher. He was not backward in administrating corporal punishment, so much so that one day he had a mutiny on his hands. The pupils rebelled, ran out of the school and locked him in. Mr Hayden could be seen in the window of the school threatening and pleading that the door be unlocked. The final outcome can easily be imagined . . .

There was no musical instrument to accompany the children in their singing and it was customary for the older pupils to go to the church and carry the harmonium to the school for the morning hymn and any other musical lesson.

The boundary wall of the school leading up to the church gate can still be seen with the coping worn smooth by the children running along the top of it.

What we now call the Summer Holidays were often referred to as Harvest Holidays. It was a period of several weeks in which attendance at school was often very poor as all the family, but more especially the older children, were kept at home to assist with the harvest.

A move was made to a Temporary Room at Pitcot granted by Lady Dunraven in November, 1863, until the new school room was finished. The building was not occupied until March, 1865. This temporary room was too small for the number of children though much better ventilated than the old one. In May, 1863, the School Log records—'Scarlet fever broke out in the school in consequence of which the school was obliged to close until the 3rd of July, even then it was raging fearfully in the village.' Remembering that the school room at this time was admitted to be too small for the numbers attending it is easy to see how quickly this outbreak assumed epidemic proportions.

The new school, built in the centre of the village, was constructed of local stone, including the stone known as 'Sutton Stone'. A cottage was also provided for the Head Master.

Mr E. Hayden. Head Master, 1863-1870
(This photograph was kindly sent from
America by Mr T. M. Rea the great
grandson of Mr Hayden.)

Mrs Draper, School sewing mistress and
Dame School mistress, who kept the
Greyhound Inn.

Site of the first school in the parish, known locally as The Plantation. Outside the wall is the tree planted by Mr Hayden the first Head Master.
(*Now purchased and preserved by the Community Council.*)

St. Brides Major School and School House.

Behind the school were separate wash houses and W.C.'s which were flushed only at weekends by the caretaker, and only then if there was sufficient water in the storage tanks which were supplied by rainwater from the roof.

In the early days very few books were available and a great deal of learning was done from large coloured pictures hung on the walls. If a pupil was proficient enough to write with a pen and ink he would be given special lessons in copperplate writing. The younger pupils used slates and slate pencils.

In 1874 it was noted that the school 'received a supply of inkwells and had them inserted into desks. A decided change for the better over the moveable inkbottles previously used.'

Extracts from School Log

1887 *July 1st:* 'Half day holiday. Children's services required to procure water for their houses; the parish water supply being exhausted.'

1888 *May 13th;* 'Wind again in the east. Rooms full of smoke.'

1888 *July 3rd;* 'There was a violent storm during the night, with the result that many children were absent searching the beach for wreckage.'

1889 *July 24th;* 'School closed two days to watch sham fights of the Volunteers on the Downs.'

1891 *Jan. 30th;* 'Large number of boys have gone "beating the bush" for the keepers, consequently no school was held this afternoon.'

1893 *July 16th;* 'Lady Dunraven gave the schoolchildren a treat at Dunraven Castle to commemorate the marriage of the Duke of York to Princess May.'

1897 *May 24th;* 'The Methodists are giving a treat this afternoon to the Band of Hope children. Nothing was known until this morning.'

1900 *May 21st;* 'The school received a holiday in order to celebrate the relief of Mafeking.'

1901 *March 11th;* 'The children in Div. III will accompany me to an elevated spot near the church from which mountains, tableland and valleys may be seen. A lesson on mountains will be given 3.15-4 p.m.'

1903 *March 19th;* 'The school closed because of diptheria.' The school did not reopen until May 4th.

1909 *July 19th;* 'The school will be closed tomorrow. The upper children will visit the Pageant in Cardiff.'

1911 *July 19th;* 'The boys' garden plots and the girls' flower gardens garden look very well. The boys and girls intend competing in the Dunraven Flower and Vegetable Show which is to be held in Dunraven Park on August 7th.'

1915 *January 7th;* 'Admitted five Belgian refugees into school.'

1918 *June 18th;* 'A number of children have gone to Bridgend to see the tank, consequently the attendance is poor.'

1919 *Sept. 18th;* 'By consent there was a public meeting held in the school in connection with the proposed erection of a memorial Parish Hall.'

1931 *Feb. 6th;* 'There is a half holiday this afternoon when a children's party will be held; and the children will be presented with gifts bought in consequence of the generosity of an old boy of the school, Mr G. Francis, of Boston, U.S.A., who sent the Head Teacher £30 for the purpose.'

1931 *Sept. 17th;* 'School outing to Cardiff. The children had a good dinner and tea, and visited the cinema, the expenses being covered through the generosity of Mr G. Francis.'

1936 *Jan. 30th;* 'There is a school holiday to take the whole school to see the pantomime 'Aladdin' at the New Theatre, Cardiff. Lunch and tea provided by Messrs David Morgan, The Hayes. The expenses were defrayed out of the George Francis Trust Fund.'

1937 *June 2nd;* 'Head Teacher absent from school attending Public Enquiry at Bridgend re proposed road widening in St. Brides Major.'

1939 *Sept. 4th;* 'It has been announced publicly over the wireless, that owing to the outbreak of war, all schools are to be closed until further notice.'

1939 *Sept. 11th;* 'School reopens. The children have been instructed to carry their gas masks to school. They will be trained to put them on quickly.'

1940 *June 28th;* 'We have had an air raid every night this week and children have been deprived of their usual sleep.'

1940 *Sept. 30th;* 'There have been many air raids during this month and the children have been dispersed on each occasion as recommended by the Director of Education; the work resumed as soon as possible after the all clear.'

1940 *Nov. 15th;* 'The new children evacuees from London are settling down nicely and are becoming quite friendly with the local children.'

1944 *August 14th;* 'Miss David retires.'

1944 *August 31st;* 'Mr T. A. Morgan, Head Master, retires.'

1945 *June 15th;* 'P.C. Elliot gave a talk to the children on the danger of touching unusual objects on the beach which may be beach mines or bombs.'

1945 *July 9th;* 'The new flushing system for lavatories alterations of the water system and fixing of an inside tap and wash basin have now been completed.'

1946 *Oct. 7th;* 'The electricity meter has now been fitted, so the school is now completed equipped with electic light.'

ST. BRIDES MAJOR SCHOOL GROUP ABOUT 1913.
Back Row: H. Benjamin, E. Llewellyn, H. Rowe, B. Sharrat, H. Bevan, I. Atyeo, W. Powell, D. David, O. Atyeo, W. Llewellyn, I. David, S. Bevan; *Middle Row:* N. Rowe, O. Atyeo, L. John, J. Thomas, P. Williams, P. Peake, I. Speak, ... W. John, A. Sharratt, P. Mitchell, J. Phillips, A. Bowen; *Seated:* M. Powell, A. Thomas, L. Watkins, E. Howe, G. Thomas, M. Smith, M. Jury, B. Bevan, B. Williams, S. Dixon, M. Miles.

ST. BRIDES MAJOR CHOIR, 1908.
(Conducted by Mr Wheeler)
Back Row: T. Dixon, E. Wheeler, E. Osborn, A. Osborn, G. Lloyd, M. David, H. Pearce, J. Sharratt; *Second Row:* Mr Wheeler, T. McDonald, H. Osborn, L. Ace, T. Williams, V. Dixon, T. David, G. Miles, W. Williams; *Third Row:* A. Griffiths, M. Lloyd, E. Dixon, L. Lewis, R. Lloyd, A. David, G. Lloyd, L. Lloyd, Mrs Wheeler, E. Davies; *Seated:* M. Lloyd, J. Wheeler, B. Hopkin.

70

1950 *Sept. 4th;* 'All children of age group eleven plus transferred from today to Pencoed Secondary School.'

1952 *June 5th;* 'School meals will now be provided from the Llantwit Major School.'

1954 *July 8th;* 'A half holiday given on the occasion of the visit by Princess Margaret to open the Sunshine Home for Blind Babies in Southerndown.

1963 *Nov. 12th;* 'The Parent Teachers' Association was formed.'

1964 *April;* 'During the Easter holidays individual flush toilets and washbasins were fitted by Glamorgan County Council.'

1966 'Electric fire being installed in two classrooms.'

1969 *March 18th;* 'John Morgan of Cardiff, Bldrs. moved on to the new school site.'

1970 *Jan. 6th;* 'New Term begins in the New School.'

1970 *Oct. 10th;* 'Official opening of the new school by Colonel M. H. Maxwell and dedication by the Archbishop of Wales.'

During the time I was at school the Head Master was a Mr Wheeler, a native of the Forest of Dean, his wife, a native of North Wales, taught Welsh generally and needlework to the girls. Mr Wheeler was a good churchman and was choirmaster and organist. He was highly respected by everyone in the parish and although a strict disciplinarian he was loved by his scholars and their parents. His two sons Joseph and Eric were pupils in the school and had no differential treatment. Joseph later became organist in Dublin Cathedral. Eric served in the Glamorganshire Yeomanry.

Let it be understood that all the children were not little angels and Mr Wheeler had a definite way of dealing with the unruly. If the occasion arose which demanded corporal punishment, he would administer it with a cane and such was the man that the offender suffered more shame than pain. There was a humorous side for the pupils who were not on the receiving end of the cane because Mr Wheeler wore loose starched cuffs and when he used the cane these cuffs would slide down and fly off the end of the cane, sometimes lodging on the high window ledge. If a chastised child went home and complained to his parents he had been caned it was of no avail as 'Master', as he was known to everyone, was like a father to all his children. Several girl scholars, when they reached school leaving age, stayed on as teachers of the infants, and one, Miss Margaret David (affectionately known as Maggi Dai) commenced teaching in 1897 and continued until retiring in 1944.

I recall two incidents on the trip to see the Pageant in 1909, when the horse-brake broke down and we were unable to get home until five

The bell tower from the Old School salvaged from the debris and erected in the garden of Rose Cottage, Penylan Road, St. Brides Major.

o'clock in the morning. The first was that my mother having prepared picnic lunches for myself and my sisters also included a banana each, and, during the journey, a fat girl sat on my lunch packet and squashed it flat. The other concerned the lady teacher who accompanied us. Her umbrella caught in a overhanging branch as we went down a lane and, as it jerked up the handle caught her under the chin and nearly choked her.

The surname of one of the Belgian refugee families was Vrijdaghs. The youngest of the three brothers, Edouard, I kept in touch with for many years after their return to Antwerp. The elder two, Jean and Gillette, were too old to attend school and had jobs in Bridgend, where they would cycle every morning. One morning they collided on the hill leaving St. Brides and were subsequently teased with the nursery rhyme about Jack and Jill. These nicknames, so close to their real names, stuck all the time they were in St. Brides.

One boy, by the name of George Francis, the son of a valet to the old Earl of Dunraven and who was living in the village, ran away from home and went to America. Later he opened a restaurant in Boston and made a great deal of money. He never forgot his old school days and, making his will, left money for the school children. The following is a copy of the letter received by the Head Master, Mr T. A. Morgan.

151, West Concord St.,
Boston,
Masachuetts,
U.S.A.
Sept. 3rd, 1930

To The Schoolteacher,
St. Brides Major,
Bridgend, S. Wales.

Dear Sir,

I am a former pupil of the school at St. Brides Major and remember something of the condition of the school children. In those days the only benefactress was the Countess of Dunraven. Since her decease, I understand nothing has been available for the children.

Having arrived, at the age of 82, in making my will, I am desirous of instituting a permanent fund to be known as the George Francis Fund for the benefit of the school children. While it will not be elaborate, in my opinion the income from it will be from £400 to £600 annually. It is my intention that two picnics be provided each year, one at Christmas, and one at Midsummer. I have instructed my trustees to appoint a committee of two to have charge of these affairs. This committee to consist of the Schoolmaster and the Government Inspector of Schools, if possible.

Owing to my physical condition it is impossible for me to travel and personally attend to this matter, therefore, I would invite your assistance as schoolteacher to furnish me with the details regarding the number of scholars and teachers in the school and also with any facts which you may think it necessary for me to have.

Thanking you for an early reply,
I am yours very truly,
Signed. George Francis

Mr Morgan the headmaster replied, furnishing the information requested, and the pupils of the school have enjoyed the benefit from this gift to this day. Although originally promising an income of £400 to £600 he was persuaded by his employees to make another will, in which his secretary received a large sum of money, and her several children also benefited. The final amount was never defined owing to the fact that an amount was divided between the school and the upkeep of his grave in America.

Modern St. Brides Major

The houses along the west side of Ewenny Road were the first to be built, as also were those around the corner into Southerndown. The new estate to the north and west of the new school is very recent as is the school itself. Along the east side of the Ewenny Road there are now private houses on the site of the old school.

The school has never strayed far from the centre of the village. This central position is not only in the literal sense, but the school has always been, and still is, a place where ex-pupils return to frequently to attend the various social activities which go on. The Annual Sports Day is well attended every year and the ladies of the parish use the school as a weekly meeting place as did their mothers and grandmothers. The Parish Council (now Community Council) hold their monthly meeting there. The school itself has, in addition to a tarmac area immediately surrounding the school, a large grassed playing area.

Mr Thomas Ambrose Morgan, a native of Cilgerran, Pembrokeshire, was headmaster in St. Brides School from 1914 until 1944. A stained glass window was dedicated by the Dean of St. Davids in memory of Mr Morgan at St. Llawddoga Church, Cilgerran. The theme of the window is 'Calling of the first two disciples' with Jesus walking by the sea of Galilee towards the fishermen brothers, Peter and Andrew. As a parallel to the fishermen in the main theme, two small panels depict the unique local industry of the coracle fishermen of Cilgerran. One shows them carrying their coracles to the river and the other depicts them in their coracles at the bend of the river with the castle on the hill above. The Chairman of the Community Council, representing the Parish of St. Brides Major, attended the dedication service.

Wells and Water

Before the Mid Glamorgan Water Board built the existing pumping station near the Ogmore Mill Farm, the problem of drinking water was a great source of worry during the dry spell in the summer months. Villagers were dependent on the wells and underground cisterns where roof water was stored. The keeping of pigeons was frowned upon because cottagers who had large underground cisterns which were fed with rain water from the roof had no means of filtering. This often caused some bad feeling between neighbours.

A favourite way of carrying water from the wells was by means of a yoke. This was a frame, of ash or elm, cut and shaped to fit around the neck and over the shoulders from which two buckets were suspended by chains, thus relieving the arms of the weight.

Pitcot Pool is fed by surface water and by springs and was used before the days of piped water was a blessing to farmers and cottagers alike for domestic and animal purposes.

The farmers would bring their water carts to the Pool and convey water to their stock in the fields. These water carts were made up of a huge barrel on wheels, pulled by a horse. This would be backed into the Pool and the farmer would fill it with a bucket. It often happened that the cart would be backed in deep to make the work easier for the filler, but when it came to pull out, sometimes it proved too heavy for the horse. Now came the question, knock out the bung to lighten the load but perhaps lose the bung—or drop into the water and fetch another horse to assist. The cottagers used the pool water to irrigate their gardens and during the summer evenings men, women, and children could be seen carrying water in all kinds of utensils.

Where there is a spring there has to be an outlet, and there is an outlet from Pitcot Pool but it does not travel more than a couple of hundred yards before disappearing into the ground at the back of the old Vicarage. The reason for this is an underground crevice running down through the village. This was called by the old people Avon Dawel (Silent River) and, until recent years, many dwellings and the school were dependent on this crevice for disposal of sewage.

It is very rare to find such a valley as St. Brides Major, with a watershed on either side, without a brook or stream running through the valley. This is unseen natural drainage.

The Mid. Glamorgan Water Board was formed in 1921 and the undertaking was vested in the Welsh National Development Authority on 1st April, 1974, in accordance with the Water Act 1973 and now forms part of the Glamorgan Water Division whose H.Q. is at Swansea.

The Schwyll springs issue from the Carboniferous Limestone on the axis of the Cardiff to Cowbridge anticline at a point where the formation outcrops near the Ewenny River, about two miles from the sea. Most of the springs appear in the immediate vicinity of the pumping station and, in earlier days, formed the Schwyll Pool.

The exact location and area of the gathering grounds are not known but it has been suggested that the catchment was in two parts. The one, in the area between the axis of the anticline and the outcrop of the Millstone Grit to the North and East, is local. The other is distant and to the North. It is known that water enters the fissured limestone outcrop in South Breconshire and it is possible that some then passes beneath the South Wales Coalfield to the East/West fissures of the Cardiff to Cowbridge anticline, and thence to Schwyll.

The behaviour of the springs in alternating dry and wet weather is consistent with the suggestion that there are both local and distant catchments.

The springs were first used for public water supply in 1872 by the Bridgend Gas and Water Co. The water was pumped from the Schwyll Pool direct to Bridgend by plunger pumps driven by mill wheels. Later, new pumps driven by gas engines were installed and were used until about 1932.

During this time an engineer named Mr David Rees of Brackla Street, Bridgend used to walk to his work at Schwyll by crossing the moors near Verville and was always accompanied by his bulldog. Mr Rees having to work late one night did not wish his dog to walk all the way to Bridgend and back again in the morning so he made a comfortable bed for it in the engine room and walked home alone, but alas, on returning to Schwyll the following morning, he was shocked to find his dog dead. It had died from gas poisoning generated during the night.

The present pumping station was brought into use in 1932 as a supplemental source for the Mid Glamorgan area as a whole. By a system of booster pumps, it was possible to transport water from Schwyll to higher levels of the mining valleys when the local upland sources are badly affected by dry weather. The water is collected from a suction well constructed over one of the main fissures. The well was sunk into the rock a little behind the cliff face from which the main springs issued. As the water passes from the well into the raw water tanks a dose of chlorine is added to kill any bacteria and before being passed into the public supply the chlorine content is automatically reduced to a level which produces no taste by the application of Sulphur Dioxide. The water is also fluoridated under strictly controlled conditions which are constantly monitered.

There are a number of wells throughout the Parish, some of which were in daily use up to 1926, when water was piped to the village. There were four wells in the village of St. Brides Major. One was on the village green opposite the Farmers' Arms but was out of use and covered with a huge stone slab. Two wells were side by side alongside Pitcot Pool. One of them was filled in during a road widening scheme and the remaining one, which can still be seen, had a heavy iron pump and was constantly in use. It is closed now as it was no longer required for water purposes and became a danger to children. Another well was in the corner of the field opposite the Fox & Hounds. This well was condemned and covered over with concrete in 1909, the reason being that it was no longer fit for drinking as it was suspected that water was seeping down from the Churchyard above.

Adam's Well is situated downstream from the stepping stones at Ogmore Castle.

Fynnon Dewi (Davids Well) is on the Common on the cliff edge at the end of the Cymdda wall at Southerndown. This was reputed to have medicinal value as a cure for rheumatism and many came to drink the water.

Jacob's Well can be found near a bend in the Alun river under Castle-upon-Alun, and it is said that the water from this well was the finest in the district for butter making.

Ruth's Well is an open well about 150 yards upstream from the Ford at Pont-y-Brown.

Another well is on Schwlac road and was stone built. A young steer in attempting to obtain a drink, fell and could not extract itself from the well with fatal result. This well is now covered and has a heavy manhole cover fixed on top.

A finely preserved well is in Pant Marie Flanders and many ramblers enjoy the lovely cool and fresh water. It is now classed as an ancient monument. The inhabitants of Heol-y-mynydd were once dependent on this well for their drinking water.

Last but not least is the Witches' Well which is near the wood behind Little Norton. Not much is known of this well, but it is said to be haunted.

Dunraven

Dunraven Castle, now demolished, was a beautiful landmark. A fine building and, although of no historic value, it was the site of the first stone castle built by Arnold Butlier. The castle being given to Dunraven by the Lord of the Manor of Ogmore for services rendered in defence of Ogmore Castle.

Although, as stated the Castle of Dunraven as a building was of no historic value, it is written that the site is classed as being 'one of the strongest fortresses in these islands'. Having been guarded on the land side by a triple entrenchment from one side of the peninsular to the other, and the other two sides defended by steep sea cliffs so that the place must have been of considerable strength and secure defence. The ancient Welsh name of Dunraven is Dundryfan which signifies the triangular fortress. It was the principle residence of the ancient Princes of Soluria and of Bran ap Llyr and his renowned son Caradoc ap Bran (The Great Caractacus). A nearby farm has been named Cae Caradoc (Caradoc's Field) after this great man. Dunraven is occasional mentioned in a very old manuscript called Bonedd-y-Saint, a document which gives, as its name imparts, brief memoirs of Primitive British Christians.

In the past the life of the village of St. Brides Major had always been centred around Dunraven. About fifty per cent of the inhabitants were employed either in the Castle or on the Estate permanently. Those who did not live at the Castle lived in houses in the village owned by the Dunraven Estate, and there was always the fear that should the tenants lose their jobs they would also lose their houses. But this was almost unknown.

The outdoor staff consisted of four gamekeepers, four forresters, four gardeners, a number of stone masons, carpenters, plumbers, and painters. The head gardener lived at Seamouth Lodge while the under gardeners, together, with the head forrester and chauffer, lived in the Bothy at the Stables.

'The Family', on their periodical visits to Dunraven from Ireland would bring with them their personal servants such as ladies' maid, footman and butler. These would be assisted by the permanent staff at the

Caroline Countess of Dunraven

Castle. It was always a great occasion when the 'Family' were coming from Ireland. All the tenants would be notified days before and were instructed to fix flags and bunting on their houses along the route.

In preparation for the annual shoot, the head gamekeeper would come to the village to obtain broody hens to put to sit on pheasants' eggs. For every hen he would pay half-a-crown. He also paid one shilling for every pheasant nest reported to him if discovered near a public footpath.

During the shoot, the gentry from the district would be invited to take part and the keeper would recruit beaters from the Parish. Although I never took part in beating I know for a fact that many a cottage table was graced by a special dish during that week. The method used was if a bird was wounded and brought down and not recovered, a mental note of the area was made by the beaters who would return after dark and collect it.

Prior to the 1914-18 War and again between the two wars (1939-45) the Dunraven Horticulture and Flower Show was held in the Castle Grounds. As children we would go along the fields gathering wild flowers and grasses to enter in our 'special classes', while there was great competition among the cottagers for the best produce etc. An interesting competition in the 'Show' was the Children's Handwriting. During Mr Wheeler's time as Headmaster at the village school he was very keen that all his scholars should have a good hand. This can be seen to this day as all his old scholars have excellent handwriting.

On the day of the show the Castle Walks were open to the public. These walks were immaculately kept and gave access to the 'Tower', called The Bower, which had a glass roof and housed exotic plants, and on to the Summer House, a circular thatched resting place on the way down to the beach known as Temple Shore. These days the walks are overgrown but one can still make one's way along them and enjoy the beauty of the coastal scenery as far as Witches Point. Here the bathing is dangerous due to currents. Approached from the shore there are some fine prawning pools at the Point. The Castle Walks are now being restored by the Glamorgan Coastal Heritage.

About seventy five yards inside the entrance gate to Dunraven Castle grounds at Seamouth Lodge and about four yards on the sea side of the

Dunraven Castle from the air. Showing cliffs and beautifully laid-out gardens.

Dunraven Bay, showing the Castle, Stables, Lodge, Park and Twyn-y-Wrach.

Dunraven Castle (front) facing South.

roadway is an oak post upon which was fixed a bronze plate bearing the following inscription:-

'This marks the place where an arrow fell
shot by Sir Ralph Frankland Payne Galway,
November 6th, 1911.
From the tower of Dunraven Castle.'

Unfortunately this plate was torn off in 1972 by vandals and was lost, but a duplicate plate has been erected by the Heritage Coast Project.

The Seamouth Cafe was originally the Dunraven Castle laundry, where all the castle laundry was done by resident laundry maids. The method of mangling the clothes here was by using a hugh wooden platform upon which the wet clothes were laid out. A box of similar size on wooden rollers, and filled with heavy stones or pebbles, would be winched by chains across the articles and the water drained out to a channel alongside. The box would then be wound back and the semi-dry clothes hung out in the drying ground. I remember seeing this method in operation on many occasions. A mangle of this description can be seen today in St. Fagans Welsh Folk Museum.

In 1886 the Duke and Duchess of Teck, with their daughter Princess May, visited Dunraven (Princess May later married George V and became Queen Mary). One Sunday morning during their stay at the castle they attended service at the Parish Church and heard the banns of marriage called for William Bevan of this parish and Isabella Scott of Abroath, County Angus, Scotland. On returning to the castle the Duchess enquired who was the Scottish girl whose banns of marriage she had heard called in church that morning. When told the girl was the head housemaid at the castle she asked to see her and congratulated her. William Bevan and Isabella Scott became my parents.

The Duke, who was interested in the rock formation in the bay, one day discovered the imprint of a human foot in a large piece of rock near the Dancing Stones. With labour from the Castle he had the stone whittled down to a portable size and took it away with him. I wonder what became of it? During their stay they would go for long walks along the cliffs and down to the shore at Ogmore. One day the Duchess slipped and her feet got wet. They went up to Sutton Farm, kept at that time by a brother and sister, Evan and Jenny David. There the Duchess took off her stockings and put on a pair of knitted woollen stockings belonging to Jenny and stayed to tea with Welsh Cakes made by Jenny.

On another occasion, Princess Mary found her room to be chilly so put a match to the fire which was always laid. Much to her alarm the

Rear of Dunraven Castle, facing north.

Dunraven Laundry, now Seamouth Cafe.

The picturesque thatched cottage at Dunraven Bay, 1908.

smoke from the fire billowed into the room. She immediately rang for help and my mother went to her assistance and saw what was the cause of the trouble. The grate, which was known as a register type, had a hinged flap which closed the flue completely. My mother opened this flap and the smoke immediately drew up the chimney. Princess May seeing what had been done exclaimed—'is that all the blooming thing wanted'.

The Blue Lady

One cannot mention the name of Dunraven without someone asking about the 'Blue Lady' of Dunraven.

My mother as stated was housemaid at the castle and, during the summer and winter months, the only illumination was by oil lamps and candles. She told me that many times she had made a night-time inspection inside the castle as part of her duties and many nights she had walked along the dark stone passages, at the witching hour, with only a candle in a large candlestick. She admitted that she was always a little frightened but was cheered by the thought that her only companion, the caretaker, was in the building. Although she had heard about the ghost, she never saw it.

84

During the First World War, when the castle was a Red Cross hospital, two nursing sisters were asleep in a bedroom when one of them awoke and in the room, faintly illuminated by moonlight, she saw a ghostly female figure dressed in a light blue flowing gown moving slowly across the room towards the closed door. She passed through leaving behind a distinct scent of Mimosa. The nurse woke her companion and related her experience and was quite definite at what she had seen.

This is not an isolated case when the apparition has appeared. But one interesting thing about these visitations is that the distinct scent of Mimosa has always been left behind.

Dunraven Castle Lodges

The first driveway to Dunravan Castle from the County road leading to Wick was about seventy five yards south of the present entrance.

The gate keepers' lodge was a picturesque round thatched cottage known locally as Ty Cobbin and occupied by John Winchcombe and his wife Jane. Although the lodge was on the main road it was a lonely spot and at the sound of footsteps or the clip clop of a horse Mrs Winchcombe would be at her little wooden gate ready to talk to someone and glean a little news or gossip. Later Mr and Mrs Winchcombe moved out of Ty Cobbin to live in a cottage situated behind the church and called Tyn-y-Fynwent.

A new driveway was later opened and a new keepers' lodge was built of coloured brick and timber set back in a wide entrance with two huge pillars on either side surmounted with heavy stone balls on each. This was named Pant-y-Groes and was occupied by George Boucher and his wife and two daughters—Edith and Elizabeth. George Boucher was employed on the Home Farm at Slade in Southerndown.

The southern lodge was at Cwm Mawr. The driveway started at Sealand Farm and the lodge was occupied by the head gamekeeper. It was here that game birds were reared and venison prepared for distribution. Mr Edwards, the head gamekeeper, upon his retirement moved to Pant-y-Groes and the lodge at Cwm Mawr was demolished, so too is Pant-y-Groes.

The northern lodge was at Seamouth and was the home of the head gardener, Mr John Sim, his wife and daughter. This lodge is stone built and constructed in a special design of stone walling known as 'snail creep'. This building has been well maintained and preserved.

The Grand Lodge is situated half-way between Pant-y-Groes and the Castle Stables. This is a picturesque building in the form of two miniature castles connected by an archway over two high gates. These gates were always kept shut and secured with two long movable iron hooks. The keeper of this lodge was Miss Jane Massey.

Miss Massey's father came over from Ireland with the Dunraven family and when he died, 'Jinny', as she was known to all her many friends, lived on in the lodge with her dog 'Sailor'. She made friends with one of the deer which roamed the park and to this animal she would talk and give food. At night the only sound to be heard at Grand Lodge was the rustle of small creatures in the undergrowth and the hooting of owls in the surrounding trees.

When my mother lived at the castle she would walk up to the lodge whenever possible to chat with Jinny. She kept up the friendship after she was married and living in the village. I remember going with my mother many a time to visit Miss Massey. It was a very weird walk in the dark, down the long driveway and, after what would seem an endless journey, a little light would become visible—this would be the lamplight in Jinny's living room. Her only brother had been lost at sea and I remember the little sailor doll she had hanging on her dresser. Miss Massey's only supply of water was from an underground manhole supplied by a spring about twenty-five yards from her front door. Her general food supplies were obtained from the castle. These she had to collect in all weathers, taking a short cut across the park and through a wood. The pathway through this wood is still known today as 'Jinny's Walk' by many of the older inhabitants.

Jinny's nearest neighbour was at Durvol Farm which is situated about a quarter of a mile from the lodge and was the Home Farm for the castle and once occupied by the forefathers of Lord Ogmore.

About a quarter of a mile due south from Durvol is a well, which was the main source of water supply to the castle. This well was worked by the 'old world' method—the pump being driven by a donkey in a circular walk. The old donkey house still stands on Dunraven Park.

A fine herd of deer roamed the park until recent years and originated from an estate called Clearwell in Gloucestershire. This herd was kept in proportion by a yearly shoot and the venison distributed among the tenants and workmen of the Dunraven Estate.

Wreckers of Dunraven and Shipwrecks on the Coast

In the old days a wrecked vessel was welcomed by the inhabitants along the coast who would rob any member of the crew alive or dead. If a stricken vessel had been lured to its doom by false lights or beacons there would be no survivors for fear they would give evidence.

The people living along the coast between Dunraven and Nash Point had long had the reputation for deliberately wrecking the sailing ships of the day. Their favourite ploy being to put lanterns on sheep and oxen thus confusing the unfortunate sailors. The leader of the wreckers in the area was known as Mat of the Iron Hand, so called because he had a hook in place of a hand. Many years before Walter Vaughan, the Lord of Dunraven and magistrate, had ordered the seizure of Mat for a misdemeanour and in the ensuing struggle Mat lost his hand in a knife thrust. Apart from Mat, who was the most notorious of the wreckers ashore, there were pirates afloat too, such as the pirate Colyn Dolphyn and others, lying in wait for the Bristol bound East Indiamen and these ships had a hard time making passage up channel.

In 1737 the square rigged *Pye* and the brig *Priscilla* homeward bound with tobacco and general merchandise were driven ashore at Nash Point. Between three hundred and four hundred persons assembled each night until their treacherous work was finished and both vessels stripped bare. The small local preventative force being quite inadequate to face the mob.

A similar fate befell the *Indian Prince* of Bristol in 1752. Homeward bound from Guinea with rum, sugar, cotton, ebony and elephant tusks, the vessel was stranded near Start Point, off Llantwit Major. Some of the looters who descended on these wrecks came from far inland villages.

In 1821 a Captain Thomas Carder was found naked and stripped by looters. He was buried at Wick. His vessel the *Hebe* had been battered to pieces under the cliffs at Dunraven with the loss of all hands. The unruly element of looters who had gathered around the wreck were bravely resisted by the Rev. Morgan of St. Brides Major and other responsible persons. But as darkness fell the defenders were hopelessly outnumbered and the vessel was completely stripped of its cargo.

In 1831 the wooden steam packet *Frolic* went aground on Nash Sands, bodies were washed ashore several months later. A General was aboard and the loss of such a high ranking military man caused such an outcry that it led to the building of a pair of lighthouses on Nash Point. Although one of these is not in use the other, with a powerful modern light, is still a prominent feature in the channel.

In 1883, the *James Gray* was wrecked on the south side of the dreaded Tusker Rock with the loss of twenty four lives and it is said that the cries of the poor people on board could be heard by the helpless people on shore. It must be remembered that at that time there was only one lifeboat between the west of Wales and Barry, and that was unservicable.

In 1886, the Bristol Channel was swept by a hurricane causing a heavy loss of life and the loss of numerous vessels.

On the night of October 15th, 1886, the ship *The Ben-y-Glo*, bound for Singapore from Penarth, ran aground at Nash Point. People from miles around, including Cowbridge and Bridgend, went to plunder the wreck. When the police searched for a roll of canvas known to have been stolen they were unsuccessful because it had been hidden in a culvert at Llandow. Many of the ships ropes too, were never found, farm workers had hidden them in furrows when ploughing. In Marcross are the remains of a stone cottage known as the Ben-y-Glo Cottage, so named because a large amount of tobacco was found buried in the garden. This was supposed to have come from the ship. There was also a tramp in the Monknash area nicknamed Ben-y-Glo because of the amount of plunder he had taken from the ship and was never caught. Although the ship was a total wreck the captain was advised to take his crew to a nearby inn to try to obtain food and hot drinks. While they were there the villagers returned to the stricken vessel and ransacked part of the cargo. Lord Dunraven however sent food to the ship's crew and invited them to the castle. There they presented him with the ship's bell and binnacle. These were always to be seen, highly polished, in the castle until recent times when the castle was demolished. They were then sent to the home of the present Lord Dunraven in Ireland.

The Marryat, a vessel wrecked off this shore gave its name to one of the early cafes in Ogmore-by-Sea. Timbers from the Marryat and some of the salvaged superstructure was erected at a later date and used as the headquarters of the contractor when laying the first sewerage scheme. On the conclusion of the contract the building was converted into a cafe and run by a Miss Webber and it remained as such for many years.

In 1886 *The Malleny* was yet another victim of the dreaded Tusker Rock. She was a Portuguese vessel and was lost with all hands. The remains of this vessel could be seen between the rock and the shore until 1979 when they were blown up by the military. Bodies of the seamen of

The wreck of the *Ben-y-Glo*, 1886.

The Malleny were washed up on the shore at Southerndown, Marcross and St. Donats and grave stones were erected in these churchyards to their memory. One is struck by these gravestones because in the days of old it was the custom, on this coast notorious for its wreckers, to show small pity or charity to the drowning or the drowned. Here we have the simple confession and atonement of one generation for another written on a stone. On September 8th, 1886, a Edwin Waters was paid off his ship *The Malleny* in Amsterdam. His family at home in Appledore did not know this and when he arrived home shortly after *The Malleny* was wrecked he found them wearing mourning black. The name plate of the ship was washed up on the shore at Westward Ho, Devon. It was bought by the grandson of Edwin Waters for five shillings who took it to his home.

It was interesting to read a recent letter sent to the *Glamorgan Gazette* in which Mr Neil Brown of Cowbridge stated that he remembered his father, Mr David Brown, describing how, when the news of the wreck reached Bridgend, he 'mitched' from school and ran all the way to Ogmore-by-Sea, via the Swing Bridge and the Stepping Stones. After walking along the sands, he joined a queue of people waiting outside a building in St. Brides and paid a penny admission to view the bodies of some of the shipwrecked sailors.

Gravestone in St. Brides Major churchyard in tribute to the crew of *The Malleny*, 1886.
The remains of Peter Francis de Sorez of Goa Madras (cook) aged 44 years. Another nine crew members unrecognised.

The Greyhound Public House (now two private dwellings). It was here that the bodies of the crew of *The Malleny* were laid out for the inquest.

In 1919 the American *S.S. Lake Western* was driven ashore at Nash Cwm, there was no loss of life. She was only ten months old and she was eventually refloated and docked, with decks awash, at Barry. When the ship struck the cliff a huge hole was stove in her port side and part of the cliff face had to blasted away to enable repairs to be carried out. The first attempt was made by bricking up the hole with bricks and cement but this proved a dismal failure as the first high tide lifted the vessel against the cliff and the brickwork crushed like an eggshell. Then an ingenious method was adopted. Hundreds of empty wooden barrels were tightly packed in the holds and secured with heavy metal bands to await the next high tide. The time arrived and a tug, *The Nodsi*, standing off in the channel put a hawser aboard and the tow began. The tug ventured too far inshore, had her bottom ripped open, and became a total wreck. After further consultation another plan was put into operation. A kedge anchor, to which a tackle was secured, was made fast out to sea and a steel hawser was made fast to the ship, carried through the tackle and taken to the cliff top and then hitched to two huge steam traction engines. When the tide was at its highest these engines began to pull. The weight was so great that the two engines were rearing up on their rear wheels like two hugh monsters. However, their efforts were rewarded for the ship floated into deep water where a tug took over and towed her to Barry. The propeller boss of the wrecked tug Nodsi can still be seen on the flat rocks at Nash Cwm.

In 1920 a Portuguese schooner the *Maria José* (Viana do Castelo) loaded with pit props was driven ashore by a gale and wrecked in Dunraven Bay. It was at the mercy of hugh breakers which were crashing against the cliff sending spray over Dunraven Castle. The watchers on shore could see the crew huddled together in the stern. There was no means of getting a rope aboard from the shore and a drum with a line attached was floated from the vessel. This eventually reached the shore and a rope secured between ship and shore over which two members of the crew came ashore. In the meantime, a young member of the crew, mistaking the signals from the shore, jumped overboard and when this lad was next seen he was out beyound the vessel and was driven against the cliff face in the left hand corner of the bay. He was next seen in the centre of the bay. A human chain was formed and he was brought ashore more dead than alive. He was taken up to Dunraven Laundry (now the café) and given hot drinks and dry clothing. He made a remarkable recovery. By this time the Porthcawl Life Saving crew had arrived and, while they were fixing the breeches buoy lines, the ship was lifted by a huge wave and put ashore high on the pebbles. The grounding was so severe that the main mast snapped and came down onto two of the crew on board. One was killed instantly and the other received compound fractures of both legs. It was an agonising sight to see this injured man being brought ashore by Breeches Buoy because as the vessel rocked the rope dipped into the sea dropping him with his exposed bones and lacerated limbs covered with blood and lifting him again all washed white. After his terrible ordeal it is pleasing to know that after a time in hospital he lived to return to his native Portugal. All that is left of the schooner is her hefty oak nameboard, six feet long and three inches thick, hand carved and decorated. It hangs over the hearth in Southerndown's old inn, The Three Golden Cups, where a bar is named after the ship. Also on the wall hangs a photograph of the stranded Maria José and a contemporary report of the wreck.

The *Polenza* a German ship, taken as a war prize after the 1914-1918 War, went ashore on Wick Beach while being taken to a Bristol Channel port. She became a total wreck and was cut up, conveyed to the cliff top, and sold as scrap.

During the 1939-45 War the *Port Carreg*, a steam coaster of some eight hundred tons sailing from Cornwall to a Bristol Channel port, was rendered helpless with engine trouble during a severe storm. At the mercy of the storm she was driven ashore in Craig-yr-eos Bay. Two members of the crew struggled ashore but the remainder of the crew were lost and their bodies never recovered. The Port Carreg remained on the sand for about six months and was then refloated and taken in tow. Off Wick beach the tow parted and she ran aground on to rocks and broke her back, becoming a total wreck. The wreck was bought by two brothers from Llanelli who cut up the vessel and hauled it piecemeal up the cliff, which at this point is the highest on the South Wales coast. It is worth recording the method adopted by these two men in carrying out this salvage work. A steel hawser was secured to the keel of the ship and to a strong metal tripod on the cliff top. A carriage was attached to a winding cable. This carriage or cradle was pulled by an Austin Seven motor car engine, converted to work a hand winch. It had a five-gallon tank for a radiator and a tank the same size for petrol. From the superstructure of the ship they constructed two wooden cabins in the Cwm and their wives and children visited them. The wives would go up to Wick to do the shopping for their husbands. In wintertime the keel of the Porth Carreg can still be seen on Wick Beach.

Between the two world wars a steam trawler, name unknown, was washed ashore in Craig-yr-eos Bay, Ogmore-by-Sea. The personal belongings of the crew and their catch of fish together with the remains of

The writer and P.C. Elliot at Craig-yr-Eos Bay, Ogmore-by-Sea with the wreck of the *Porth Careg* in the background, 1939-1945.

the vessel were strewn along the water's edge, a most pathetic sight. The ribs and keel of this trawler can be seen at low water near Craig-yr-eos Bay.

During the 1939-45 War a tanker in convoy was torpedoed or mined off Nash Point with the result that all the coast from Nash to Porthcawl was covered with thick crude oil, causing havoc to fishing and wild life.

Another incident of less serious consequences took place off our coast. *The Catto*, sailing from North Wall, Dublin, to a South Wales port, sank off Dunraven with her cargo of forty-gallon barrels of Guinness Stout. Dozens of these barrels were washed up along the stretch of coast and the police and excise men prevented the unlawful use of the contents. The majority were found but some locals were perhaps cleverer than others and got away with some of the barrels. One farmer salvaged two barrels with a horse and dray from the other side of the Ogmore river. He put them up ready to tap and had invited some of his pals for a real old binge. But alas, the news leaked out and the police and excise men visited the farm. They rolled the barrels out on to the field and knocked out the bungs. The unlucky farmer had the mortifying sight of seeing a river of froth running down the field as far as the café.

In August 1965, children playing and digging in the sand on the common about fifteen yards from high water mark under Craig-yr-eos discovered a quantity of bones. The children whose father was a doctor recognised them as human bones but of an early age. It is quite possible that the bones were the remains of some unfortunate seamen washed ashore from one of the many maritime disasters of long ago and maybe were buried where the bodies were found.

In 1969 a Greek ship the *Amalia* went aground on the Nash Shelf, but was later refloated.

The latest victim claimed by the ever present Tusker Rock is the *Steep Holm*. A 532 ton dredger which struck the rock with little damage. Before salvage work got under way, a severe storm came in from the Atlantic and completely demolished the vessel—quicker than any breakers' yard could have done. The boiler and some of the heavy metal parts are still visible.

The Windermere

In 1953-54, when I was returning home from work via the coastal route, I saw a ship on the Tusker Rock. The tide being about half-way out, the rock was not visible but knowing the coast I was certain the vessel was stranded. I returned to Ogmore-by-Sea, with my daughter and son-in-law, and saw that the tide had now receded and the rock being fully exposed showed the vessel upright high and dry on the rock. With a telescope and from a vantage point near the old Sutton quarry, we were able to see the ship quite clearly and about half-a-mile up channel was a lifeboat with the crew in their yellow life jackets bobbing about in a moderate sea. Darkness was falling and visibility failing, so we returned home and tuned in the radio, via the Ilfracombe Radio, we heard the conversation and argument between the owners of the ship *Windermere*, and the tug owners in Swansea, who wanted one hundred pounds to tow the vessel off the rock. Agreement as to the charge could not be reached. During this time the Mumbles lifeboat, which was standing by, had a conversation with the ship's master telling him not to worry because 'if it came to the worse I will pull you off but if you feel her beginning to bump give her all the power you have got (which was only an auxilliary engine) and I will stand by you'. The tide rose and the *Windermere* floated clear. The lifeboat coxwain said 'good boy, I'll put my search-light skywards so follow me around the Fairy buoy'. All this in a very strong Welsh accent. This manoeuvre was carried out and the vessel got into port undamaged and without loss of life, thanks to the Mumbles lifeboat. The sailing ship *Windermere* was believed to be an Irish potato boat.

Beach Combing

There are numerous stories dealing with the wrecking of ships along the coast of Glamorgan. Fortunately with modern maritime navigational aids these tragedies have virtually ceased to exist but beachcombing is still a delight enjoyed by the people who live along the coast.

Up to the outbreak of the First World War it was a recognised thing that after a severe westerly gale the local inhabitants would, as soon as it became daylight (indeed some would be waiting on the shore before daylight) get down to the shore and collect any wreckage which had been washed up. There was an unwritten law among these people that once this salvaged wreckage had been collected and put into a pile above high water mark nobody would touch it, although there was great competition among the collectors. In these heaps could often be seen cabin doors, with brass ventilators, brass bound companion ladders and rails, sail cloth, ropes and sometimes hidden underneath would be a rum barrel.

A horse and cart would be hired or borrowed and each man's lot would be taken home. If you walked around the district today you can still see some of these doors on outside lavatories and garden sheds. The clothes line post may well be a ship's spar and the clothes prop a boat hook.

S.O.S. Message

Ever since I was a boy, having read 'Treasure Island', 'Robinson Crusoe', 'The Castaways' etc., I have always looked for a message in a bottle, but it was thirty odd years before my search was rewarded.

On Sunday 10th of December, 1939, while serving as a special constable with the Glamorgan Constabulary, I was patrolling the shore in Dunraven Bay when, in Corner Ddu, I found a pint and a half bottle containing the following message.

14th October /39	Brig Susie
Steering SW-W	N-Y 7921
Twelve days from Sandy Hook Point.	
Estimated position / 32W. 45N.	
Water short, food for two weeks.	
Mast snapped, boat leaking.	
The envelope was addressed thus:-	
Please take to the nearest Police Station N.Y.	

The above message was handed into Bridgend Police Station and a copy was sent to Lloyds and Trinity House. Being wartime nothing further was heard, but it was established that it was a genuine message.

Southerndown

In about 1820 plans were drawn for a proposed Garden City in Southerndown. The site for this development and elaborate scheme was the land between the Dunraven Hotel and the Cymdda.

These plans showed a high centre building, inside a circle, with an outer circle of buildings and dwellings. Although the plans were drawn after an extensive survey the scheme proved to be too ambitious and fell through.

In 1848 this announcement appeared in a local paper:-

FOR SALE by public auction
by Mr Robert Evans, Auctioneers, Bridgend.
Dated 7th June, 1848.
SOUTHERNDOWN in the Parish of St. Brides Major.

The Southerndown property, comprised of Lots No. 34 to 46, is beautifully situated on the Bay of Dunraven commanding extensive and delightful views of the Bristol Channel and of Dunraven Castle and Park and the adjacent splendid scenery of this romantic spot and is a favourite resort of invalids and others on account of the salubrious air and the convenience of sea bathing. The whole property affords a rare opportunity for investment.

Dunraven Bay showing Dancing Stones and Hardee's Marquee on foreshore.

These several Lots will be sold at the Wyndham Hotel, Bridgend, on the 11th July next at one o'clock in the afternoon.

(Signed) Messrs Riccard and Son, Solicitors. South Molton.

These plots of land represented the land from the Sunshine Home to the Cymdda.

Before the existing Dunraven Hotel (now the Rest Home for the Blind) was built, the original Dunraven Hotel was a low thatched building which was demolished for the present building. The Dunraven Hotel was a residential hotel and catered for a high class of visitors. The hotel ran a horse brake service between the hotel and Southerndown Road Station, primarily to convey residential visitors and their luggage.

The driver of the brake was Mr Walter Symes who lived in Dunlop Cottage, Southerndown and was well liked by the local people for his generosity in giving lifts whenever possible. He would never whip away youngsters riding on the back step, a practice I have indulged in many times. This was before the days of tarmacadam roads so when a horse-drawn vehicle passed by in dry weather a cloud of dust was left behind. In spite of the dust a stolen ride was enjoyed.

Until World War I there was, on top of the pebbles in Southerndown, a Summer House shelter built by Lord Dunraven for the use of the visiting public. This building was so abused that he had it removed but the foundations can still be seen to this day.

The Dunraven Hotel, Southerndown, 1909.

As a lad I well remember seeing painted notice boards fixed on the wall near the lodge at Dunraven Bay. One stated:-

'MIXED BATHING STRICTLY PROHIBITED'

and the other:-

'LADIES ARE REQUESTED TO BATHE ON THE EAST SIDE OF THE BAY AND GENTLEMEN ON THE WEST SIDE.'

How things have changed these seventy odd years.

On the grass, now the car park, during the summer months was a large canvas tent where trippers could obtain tea and home-made cakes, sweets and lemonade. This refreshment tent was kept by Mr William Hardee, who later built Hardee's Cafe at Ogmore-by-Sea. Later the business was taken over by Mr Dixon who lived in a little cottage called the Glouty near Pwll-y-Mer (Southerndown Pool).

Near the Glouty were two picturesque thatched cottages known as Douglas Cottages, but time has taken its toll and only the remains of the foundations are left. The Glouty was a favourite spot for the local lads to gather and play games on the common nearby and many a time I, with other lads, have been chased away by Mr Dixon for sitting on the window cill of the cottage.

Mr Dixon owned a donkey named Harkaway and it was with this donkey and a flat bottomed cart that he would remove his stock from the tent on the foreshore every night during the summer season. Mr Dixon with his donkey transport used to carry laundry baskets to and from

Southerndown Village showing The Glouty Cottage, in the foreground, and Pwll-y-Mer.

98

Southerndown Road Station for the big houses and hotels in the parish. Mr Dixon was a tall man of over six foot and always walked alongside his conveyance. He was never known to beat his donkey and his method of increasing the rate of travel was to brush the roadway behind the donkeys heels with a bass broom, which he always carried on his cart.

Further up the road from the Glouty and Douglas Cottages was the Vines. This was an old stone house which was demolished and rebuilt just before World War I.

Behind the Vines is Westfield, a long rambling stone-built dwelling, which was at one time a farm house until the land was divided into plots and put up for sale.

The post office at this time was to the rear of Seaview Cottages, now Fashoda House, the home of Mr and Mrs R. Heard. The postmistress was Miss Rowe and her father Thomas Rowe farmed Southerndown Farm. Mr Rowe was also a coal merchant, obtaining his coal from Southerndown Road Railway Station with his horse-drawn waggons.

His waggoner was a local man named William Powell, who, when the 1914-18 war broke out returned to the farm with his load of coal, stabled his horse, quarrelled with his boss, and went off in a temper to join the army. He returned home safely when the war ended.

Overlooking the Bristol Channel and the Somerset and Devon coast is the Sunshine Home for Blind Babies (recently sold). This building which proudly bears the work of the real stone masons of the period was once The Marine Hotel. A residential hotel much favoured by visitors and locals alike, the visiting golfers who, when participating in competitions found it very convenient, would find easy access to the golf course by a walk through Heol-y-mynydd. The hotel was highly recommended by the R.A.C. and the Cycling Union.

The main road from Southerndown to Ogmore at that time passed the side door of The Marine, around the back of the building. It passed the entrance gates to Glan-y-Mor, along the walls of Glan-y-Mor grounds and turned sharply westwards near the end of Green Lane, about one hundred yards east of Little West.

In 1921-22 a road improvement scheme was carried out and a new road was made. Commencing opposite the Terraces and across farm land to join up with the old road near Green Lane. A wall was built across the old road behind the Marine Hotel, near Glan-y-Mor entrance, and a new entrance to the Hotel was made by a drive in from the new road.

There is a little story connected with this road improvement. Many years ago a native of Southerndown emigrated to America. He exchanged letters with Mr William Powell of Bay House, St. Brides Major. In one of his letters Mr Powell told him of the road improvement in Southerndown. He received a reply from America asking him to try and find a large stone which the man, as a boy, had put into the wall. If Mr Powell could find it, he would like to have it built into one of the new walls. Mr Powell contacted my father who had the contract to build the new wall and told him the story. I had not long come home from the army and at that time was helping my father. Together we searched and found the stone, I cut the date 1921 into the face of the stone and we built it into the new wall leading up to the side entrance of the Marine Hotel, on the Heol-y-mynydd Road, where it may still be seen.

About five hundred yards on the Ogmore side of the Dunraven Bay, past the Dancing Stones, is the Pebble Beach and here under the cliffs is The Devil's Pool reputed to be bottomless. The local gallants being good swimmers would dive in and swim in defiance of the name and tradition. I admit to being one of the culprits.

Further along the Bay are the Caves, one is known as the Fairy Cave. These caves can only be visited at low tide and have proved highly dangerous to the uninformed visitor. About sixty years ago two young ladies from Birmingham, who were on holiday at Southerndown, visited the caves and were trapped by the incoming tide and drowned. Their little dog which was with them, swam ashore at Dunravan Beach.

On the common above the caves is Twyll-y-Gwynt (wind hole). This is a crevice in the rock connected to the caves underneath. On the incoming tide the huge waves would drive into the cave forcing the trapped air to blow up through this opening. Many a time I have thrown my cap into the top of this hole and waited for the next wave below to blow it out on-to the common.

The cliffs at Southerndown rise to a height of 150-200 feet and they are the favourite nesting place of seagulls. Unfortunately, many a young lad has lost his life or been seriously injured in the pursuit of seagull eggs.

These cliffs are made dangerous for climbers as they are composed of beds of lower lias interspersed with calcareous and argillaceous earth. The carboniferous limestone near Trwyn-y-Wych (Witches Snout or Point) is stated to be one of the finest examples in Wales.

Owing to the fact that these cliffs face south west they are thereby exposed to the fury of the Atlantic gales, especially during the winter months. During the last one hundred years the continual buffeting has altered the face of the cliffs. For example, about fifty yards south of the pebbles, at Dunraven Bay, there was a cave running under the cliff to a depth of approximately fifteen to twenty yards. This was known locally as 'Booker's Hole', but through continual cliff falls this cave has completely disappeared, the cliff at this point now being shear.

Weather Forecast

In the old days the inhabitants of St. Brides Major would forecast the weather by the sound of the sea. If one heard the sound of the returning breakers rolling the pebbles back at Seamouth (Dunraven Bay) this would signify bad weather with rain to follow from the south. But if the sea could be heard roaring at Cwter Fawr, (Pant-yr-Slade or Black Rocks) Ogmore-by-Sea, this would mean fine weather to follow from the north east.

Laverbread

The gathering or picking of Laverbread was much favoured in the old days, much more than it is today. Near Corner Ddu in Dunraven Bay is a pool in the flat rocks, measuring 20ft × 18ft and 18in deep, known as the Laverbread Pool. Here the pickers would wash sand from their collection of weed by standing astride the pool and swinging and dipping their baskets into the water, allowing the sand to wash out without losing any of the Laverbread.

Prawning

There are also some good prawning pools on the South side of Trwyn-y-Wych (Witches Point), Dunraven Bay and on the Black Rocks at Ogmore-by-Sea.

There are two places where picnickers could obtain fresh water to make their tea—at Corner Ddu, to the left of the Dunraven Bay and halfway up the cliff face there is a spring sending riverlets to fall on to the pebbles below. Sometimes it is difficult to get a good supply without getting wet due to the overhanging cliff. The problem was often solved by the person already dressed for bathing fetching the water while the others would collect driftwood for the fire.

The other source of supply was from the Pistyll. A stone spout was built into the Park Wall above the Laundry (now Seamouth Cafe). This was put there by Lord Dunraven and the water obtained by piping water from a spring inside the Park. This is no longer in use.

Jacob's Ladder

During my many talks to various local organisations, I have mentioned Jacob's Ladder and this warrants an explanation. About two hundred yards north of Little West Farm on the County Road, between Southerndown and Ogmore-by-Sea, is a valley running down to the foreshore and the black rocks, described on the Ordnance Map as Pant-yr-Slade, known by the locals as Cwter Fawr, (Big Gutter). At the bottom of this miniature valley was one of the smaller Sutton stone quarries. Men working at this quarry would climb up the valley to the cliff top by rough steps cut out in the steep bank. These steps are in constant use by visitors and ramblers. As these steps rise from the bottom of the valley skywards I have always likened them to the Biblical 'Jacob's Ladder' and this name has now been accepted by the Glamorgan Coastal Heritage Project, who have taken over its maintenance.

Lordship of Ogmore and Dunraven

Ogmore-by-Sea, as it is known today, did not exist prior to the First World War. This part of the parish was known as Sutton, taking its name from the celebrated Sutton stone quarries which were a part of Southerndown. The old maps of 1840 show three houses, the oldest being Sutton Farm House the other two were Craig-yr-Eos Farm and Sealawn. In 1878 three more buildings were added, Tusker House, Sealawn Farm and St. Margarets. By 1918 Sealawn had been renamed Slon and St. Margarets changed to Brig-y-Don. In 1958 Slon reverted to its original name of Sealawn.

The original Lordship of Ogmore consisted of land from the mouth of the River Ogmore, running eastwards towards Coychurch. It included Corntown, Ewenny, Colwinstone, Wick, St. Brides Major and the whole of the Ogmore and Garw Valleys. This Lordship was granted to William de Londres by Fitzhamon at the time of the conquest of Glamorgan in 1093. Market fairs were held at Ogmore Castle in the fourteenth century and fairs were held at Ewenny and St. Brides. The De Lundres family also held Kidwelly Castle in Carmarthen and this became their main residence.

During one of their visits to Kidwelly, they left Ogmore Castle in charge of one of their stewards by the name of Arnold Botlier and during

Ogmore Castle and Stepping Stones.

that time the castle was attacked from the sea. Botlier put up a strong resistance and forced the attackers to retreat. When De Loundres returned and learned of the gallant fight his steward had put up to defend the castle, he granted him a Knighthood and gave him Dunraven.

Dunraven was derelict at the time and Arnold Botlier built the first stone building on the site. The tenure of the Manor was to be three cups of wine, to be drank whenever the Lord of the Manor of Ogmore chanced to visit Dunraven. Three golden cups were to be included in the arms of Le Botlier.

When Dunraven Castle was demolished in recent years, the coat of arms in stone was salvaged and is now in the care of Lord Dunraven.

Portobello

On the south side of the River Ogmore, near the Bridgend to Ogmore-by-Sea road and opposite the valley leading to Heolymynydd, known as Pant Mari Flanders, is Portobello, now a modernised private dwelling. This was Portobello Hotel, Ogmore.

Mouth of the river Ogmore with Portobello House in the trees near the river and showing the old Artillery magazine.

In the days when public houses throughout Wales were closed on Sundays, if a person could prove to the innkeeper that he had travelled three miles or more he would be classed as a bonafide traveller and allowed in to partake of refreshment.

In those days the landlord of a public house would sell to his customers, tokens or checks similar to ones used today by large stores and dairies. When a workman was paid his wages he would purchase, from his favourite pub, as many of these checks as he could afford, so that when his money was spent he could always get a drink by using one of these checks.

If a man went to a public house the innkeeper would ask him if he had any money, if he had none he was shown the door, but if he could produce a token he was allowed to partake of refreshment. Here we have the old saying, 'Enough to lift the latch'. I have in my possession one of these tokens from Portabello.

The hotel being the required distance from Bridgend no doubt decided the Glamorgan Artillery to site their range near the hotel. As the majority of the members lived in Bridgend it was the practice, when the Sunday morning firing was over, to spend the rest of the day in the hotel. Many stories relate to the smuggling of drinks out to the local members, who were known to the landlord and were not bonafide travellers.

Old Sutton Farm House, Ogmore-by-Sea.

The gun, which was fired out to sea, was mounted on a heavy wooden platform and nearby was a brick-built magazine where the ammunition was kept. For many years after its abandonment by the army the magazine was used as a private dwelling, but was demolished by the Penybont Rural District Council under a clearance scheme.

Ogmore and Ogmore-by-Sea

The village of Ogmore consisted of the thatched cottages and the farm surrounding the Ogmore Castle.

There are many stories relating to the stepping stones near Ogmore Castle. They are known by many as the steps of St. Teilo, having been brought to Ogmore from the crossing of the River Ogmore near the Ford or Swing Bridge at Merthyr Mawr. One story tells how the daughter of the Lord of the Manor of Ogmore living in the castle had the stones put there so that her lover, who lived on the other side of the river, could visit her without discomfort. The stepping stones at Ogmore were well known, for it was at these stones that the Baptists in the district celebrated their Baptismal Rites. A large congregation would gather on the grass bank surrounding the ruins of the castle to witness the service which took place in the waters of the Ewenny River. The minister would wade into the water to the fourth or fifth stone and as the candidates

Sandy Mount on Slon Road and Craig-y-reos Road showing cornfields, now built upon. In foreground is waste rubble from one of the Sutton Quarries.

would walk toward him he would immerse them in the water. The candidates were prepared in the little thatched cottage nearby known as Star Cottage.

I remember being taken to Ogmore to witness one of these ceremonies when a terrible storm arose from the Atlantic, high winds accompanied by torrential rain soaking everyone present. Being of a tender age I was more interested in the number of umbrellas that were blown inside out than in the religious ceremony.

It is much favoured by the residents and visitors to walk over to Newton and Porthcawl by wading across the mouth of the Ogmore River when the tide is out.

Living in Portobello House at one time was a man by the name of Prosser who owned a flat-bottomed home-made boat and it was the custom that, when walkers returned home and finding the tide in, would walk up stream to Portobello and shout to Mr Prosser who would then launch his little craft and ferry them over for a small fee. This saved them the long walk back to Merthyr Mawr and over the stepping stones at Ogmore Castle.

The unveiling of the plaque at Ogmore-by-Sea with Sister Eulalia and Sister Naomi.

Plaque to mark a Beauty Spot

On Saturday, June 16th, 1972, a number of people gathered on a lovely part of the coast-line, on the common between Southerndown and Ogmore-by-Sea, to witness a ceremony unique in the history of the parish of St. Brides Major. It was the unveiling of a plaque to mark a place of outstanding beauty. These plaques have been distributed throughout Europe, the United States of America and parts of Great Britain. This was the third to be erected in Wales, the other two being on the Rhigos Mountain and on Llantrisant Common. It is the work of the Evangelical Sisterhood of Mary of Frankfurt, Germany, and Radlett, Hertfordshire, England, to place these plaques bearing verses from the Psalms.

The one at Ogmore-by-Sea is bilingual and is set in a block of the celebrated Sutton Stone. This block of Sutton Stone had been quarried nearby, well over one hundred years ago, and still bore the marks of the workman's drill. This stone had been brought back from the old Sawmill at Merthyrmawr where it had lain, waiting to be dressed for some architectural project.

Dr Pell-Cocks, of Ogmore-by-Sea, spoke of the beauty on our doorstep and how little thought was given to the creator of it all. He hoped this would be a reminder to all who enjoyed this scene of outstanding beauty.

The plaque was unveiled by Sister Eulalia and Sister Neomi, of the Sisterhood. The Vicar of the parish, the Rev. H. A James, carried out the dedication and closed the ceremony by pronouncing the blessing.

Mor lliosog yw	O Lord
Dy weithredoedd	How manifold are thy works
O Arglwydd	In Wisdom
Gwnaethost hwynt	Hast thou made them all
Oll mewn doethineb	The earth is full of thy riches.
Llawn yw y ddaear	
O'th gyforeth.	
Salm 104/24	Psalm 104/24

The War Years

Red Cross Hospitals

These were set up and staffed by Red Cross personnel at Dunraven Castle, Tusker House and Hardee's Cafe, Ogmore-by-Sea, during the First World War, 1914-1918.

During the Second World War, 1939-45, a great increase of membership was experienced and good medical service was given to members of H.M. Forces. Hospitals were established at Dunraven Castle, Tusker House and Brig-y-don, Ogmore-by-Sea. Many local residents helped at these establishments.

An Air Raid Warden service was formed in the parish during the period of World War II, under the supervision of the late Police Superintendent William C. May, of the Glamorgan Constabulary. Instruction would be given in the cricket pavilion at Southerndown, with posts at the pavilion and The Vicarage, St. Brides Major. When the 'red' alert was phoned from Bridgend, the wardens on duty would patrol the village blowing three short blasts on a police whistle and on the 'green' all clear they would again patrol ringing a hand-bell, which in this day and age of 'radio patrol' seems very primitive—but it worked.

The vicar, the Rev. Wills, was a great stalwart on these occasions and being the Senior Warden was given a patrol allowance to use his little Morris 8 for this purpose.

The writer's mother, Mrs Isabella Bevan, Southerndown V.A.D., 1915.

MEMBERS OF THE SOUTHERNDOWN VOLUNTARY AID DETACHMENT
(at Tusker House Hospital, Ogmore-by-Sea).
Back: Mrs Toms, Peggy Davies, Ms Gladys Wimbow, Dulcie Booker, Mrs Owen, Nellie Symes, Nancy Owen, Annie McDonald; *Middle:* Gwyneth Knowles, Eileen Bamon, Henrietta Booker, Sir E. McClean, Dr. Rocyn-Jones, Ethel Booker, Nurse Rees (village nurse); *Seated:* Gwen Miles, Mildred Powell, Eileen Knowles, Connie Bevan, Peggy Mordicai.

A.F.S.

During these times an Auxillary Fire Unit was based in Kings Hall Farm, St. Brides Major, and in the evenings the local men could be seen practising their fire fighting drill at the edge of Pitcot Pool. These men were involved in fire fighting during the heavy blitz on Swansea and surrounding areas.

Auxilliary Fireman Hubert Taylor was commended for an act of gallantry, when he rescued a number of horses from a blazing building off Wassell Square, Swansea, at great risk to himself. This courageous act was brought to the notice of His Majesty the King and published in the London Gazette on Friday, 9th May, 1941.

During an air raid the children of the village school would be dispersed to the surrounding houses to await the 'all clear' which could sometimes be heard from the siren on Bridgend Police Station. The local children also performed a special salvage campaign, each week collecting paper to be re-cycled for the war effort.

During World War II, strict precautions were taken to prevent illicit landings by enemy agents. Our coast line at Southerndown, Ogmore-by-Sea, Monknash and Marcross was deemed vulnerable and these bays were fenced off and mined. No unauthorised person was allowed on any of these beaches. The common at the river mouth was completely fenced off and land mines were laid within this boundary. These mines were inspected periodically by the army because the wind blowing the sand would occasionally expose the buried mines. During one of these inspections at Ogmore-by-Sea, carried out by an officer and an N.C.O., a tragedy occurred. Two men were seen by the local postman, Mr James Down, doing their round of inspection when the officer stepped on a mine and was blown to pieces. Apparently they had read the blue print incorrectly with this tragic result.

At Southerndown Bay the minefield was extended a short distance inside the park wall of Dunraven Castle and was enclosed by the usual barbed wire entanglements and notices were erected bearing the words, 'MINE FIELD—KEEP OUT', but to the deer which roamed the park this did not mean anything and one of them, taking a run, cleared the fence and landed on a mine. Its remains had to be cleared off the roof of the nearby lodge.

During the latter part of the war the parish became a declared military area with the Pitcot end of the village becoming a satellite airfield with airforce personnel from the R.A.F., Australia and New Zealand.

At the Ewenny end of the village, in Parc Wood, a large U.S. Army camp was established, mainly under canvas, and this was their stepping

AIR RAID WARDENS, 1939-1945.
Back Row: L. Hayden, P. C. Elliot, D. McDonald, J. Sim, G. Lewis, S. W. Bevan; *Middle Row:* Rev. D. Wills, V. Cotty, A. Morgan, J. Herbert; *Seated:* M. Miles, D. Gibbs, A. Wills, M. Bevan, Supt. W. May, —Elliot, B. Pearce, D. Jones, E. Bevan.

stone before embarking for war in the Far East. The stores and bakery for this enormous number of men was at Southerndown, alongside Seamouth Cafe and on top of the Cymdda. This was manned by U.S. coloured personnel.

Should the children of the village school be out in the playground at the time these soldiers were passing, the men would stop their ration convoy and roll tins of fruit and food among the children. Food being rationed, this was indeed a 'gift from the gods'.

A very special 'do' was held in the parish to celebrate V.E. Day when everybody gave something towards the party from their saved up rations, and this was repeated on V.J. Day.

A Welcome-Home Committee was formed during these years when the boys returning home from the war were given a concert by local talent and presented with a gift of money.

Welsh Speaking

Up to the middle of the 1800's practically all the inhabitants of the parish spoke Welsh, with the exception of a few. These were some of the staff of Dunraven, who had come to Dunraven from Limerick, Ireland. The others were men from Devon ànd Somerset who had come over to

111

the Vale to work on the land during the harvest time, met and married local girls and settled down in the Vale. These were known locally as 'Come Overs' and often had their legs pulled because it was said that once they were here they never returned. These people were good workers, good natured and made good citizens.

Radical Changes

Up to the time of the 1914-18 war a great rivalry existed in the parish, even between good neighbours. There was always that feeling 'You are all right, but you are not one of us'. So great was this antagonistic feeling that even in death a nonconformist would not be taken into the church, prior to being buried in the churchyard.

One thing which brought the children of all denominations together was the Band of Hope. Members of the Band of Hope took part in the Gymanfa Ganu when some lovely old Welsh hymns and anthems were sung in Welsh and English.

An amusing incident took place one Sunday evening when the antagonistic feeling was at a high peak. An old lady, who was blind, was being led up the road by her son to the evening service at the Baptist chapel, while some people were walking on the other side of the road in the opposite direction, evidently going to the church. The old lady stopped and in a loud voice said, 'Tom is that the old church trash passing'. As a boy I knew her well, she was a dear soul and a devout worshipper.

In recent years a dramatic change has overtaken the old parish. No longer is there rivalry between the different denominations. The Church of England and the Nonconformists, although retaining their own ideas and beliefs, live together in perfect harmony to the benefit of the community.

Some of the old farms owned by the Dunraven Estate no longer exist as such. The land has been merged into neighbouring farms and the farm houses have become private dwellings. Gone is the old school, with its fine Sutton stone work and bell tower, gone too are the old village blacksmith and bakehouse, so too has the village pump.

Modern bungalows and houses have been built, and it is sad to see some of the old relics and landmarks disappear, but one must bow to the path of so-called progress.